The Case for the Humanities

The Case for the Humanities

Pedagogy, Polity, Interdisciplinarity

Eric Touya de Marenne

ROWMAN & LITTLEFIELD
Lanham • Boulder • New York • London

Published by Rowman & Littlefield
A wholly owned subsidiary of The Rowman & Littlefield Publishing Group, Inc.
4501 Forbes Boulevard, Suite 200, Lanham, Maryland 20706
www.rowman.com

Unit A, Whitacre Mews, 26-34 Stannary Street, London SE11 4AB

British Library Cataloguing in Publication Information Available

Library of Congress Cataloging-in-Publication Data

ISBN 978-1-4758-2501-5 (cloth : alk. paper) -- ISBN 978-1-4758-2502-2 (pbk. : alk. paper) -- ISBN 978-1-4758-2503-9 (electronic)

∞ ™ The paper used in this publication meets the minimum requirements of American National Standard for Information Sciences Permanence of Paper for Printed Library Materials, ANSI/NISO Z39.48-1992.

Printed in the United States of America

I dedicate this book in memory of James R. Lawler, my academic mentor at the University of Chicago, who had a love for the humanities and a gift for sharing his passion.

Contents

Preface

Could there be a place for literature, art, history, and philosophy in our universities and in a world dominated by vocational training, science, technology, and business? The purpose of this study is to examine how the raison d'être and state of the humanities have academic but also cultural, political, societal, and existential ramifications.

The premise of this book is based on the notion that we live in a time of crisis: our technologically driven world possesses the means of its own destruction; economic and financial policies undermine the very existence of our democracy; and the postmodern, posthuman age fundamentally challenges our ability and legitimacy to conceive future ideals. In the midst of this scientific, economic, political, environmental, and existential crisis, the humanities must be valued at the level of their eminent importance.

Beyond the positive nature of physical or social science ("what is"), the humanities expand one's intellectual inquiry to examine "what ought to be." They bear an emancipatory potential that naturally generates individual and societal change through independent thinking and critical awareness—a potential to reconnect the text and the world, to recognize the link between power and truth, and to expose students to difference and otherness.

They constitute in this respect a model through which the teaching and interpretation of economics and STEM must be reenvisioned today. At stake with this reconceptualization, which calls for border-crossing and a rehabilitation of the other through critical pedagogy, is the extent to which humanity can or should be in control of its destiny.

Contrary to technical or utilitarian values and market measurements, the humanities provide students and faculty—and all citizens of the world—with the ability to struggle against any form of power that seeks to transform them into objects or instruments in the spheres of knowledge, truth, consciousness, and discourse.

Should higher education be limited to the sphere of intellectual rather than moral virtue? Should more emphasis be given to vocational benefits while liberal education is abandoned? Such changes would inevitably enhance the rise of scientific, technical, and professional academic disciplines. They would also corroborate the views of Stanley Fish: that the humanities have no contributory values, only intrinsic worth, and should thus not be regarded as instrumental to some greater good.

Beyond the notion that knowledge may be inculcated for its own sake, liberal education's societal and global significance needs to be recognized and revealed. Far more than schooling based on purely economic or technological usefulness, it is conducive to raising moral and intellectual inquiries that sharpen the critical capacities of students. The former prepares the individual for a specific task or practice that has utilitarian value while the latter demands a reflection about the students' place and responsibility in society and the world—socially, civically, and existentially.

The weakening importance of liberal education—including literature, philosophy, and history—is detrimental to preparing students and future citizens who must learn to reflect on how they should live in society and face the political, technological, and existential challenges of our times.

Given that in our postmodern and posthuman world, economics, science, and technology have been elevated to a quasi-sacred form of religion, and that cyborgs, clones, and robots have allegedly altered the human condition, what response can the humanities provide? Asking this question leads precisely to where the humanities' and humanity's fate and future are at stake and become one.

More than any other academic fields, the humanities inspire students to explore the relation between the university and society, knowledge, and power, and to develop their capacity for synthesis, critical thinking, ethical vocation, and civic participation. They are essential and far more valuable than business, economics, science, or technology because they lead us to not only question the world as it is but also how it ought to be.

The political and pedagogical implications of this interdisciplinary study thus entail a renewed criticism whose aim is to rethink the relation among higher education, society, and the world at large (politically, economically, scientifically, and technologically) and the importance of the humanities within it.

Acknowledgments

I would like to thank the Department of Languages and the College of Architecture, Arts, and Humanities at Clemson University for granting me course reductions for research and scholarship, and the Humanities Advancement Board for its generous support. This book would not have been possible without the academics who have enthused my interest in the arts and humanities and enriched my reflection on the subject: Richard Taruskin, Marika Kuzma, Basil Guy, Walter Rex, James R. Lawler, Peter F. Dembowski, Françoise Meltzer, Pierre Brunel, François Furet, Karyna Szmurlo, Leslie Williams, Michael Bérubé, and Marc Fumaroli.

It is my pleasure to express my appreciation to Cayley Balser, Kirsten Dean, Elizabeth Stansell, and Lauren Woolbright, who all contributed to the preparation of the manuscript. Finally, I wish to thank my wife, Lucile Luo, and my daughter, Madeleine, for their unyielding support.

Introduction

One of the most urgent issues confronting academia today is the perception that the humanities are unessential. Liberal arts colleges have been particularly affected by their steady decline and the surging demand for career-oriented instruction. Victor E. Ferrall attested that "over the twenty-one years between 1986–1987 and 2007–2008 the number of colleges graduating at least 90 percent liberal arts majors fell by more than half," while the number graduating 30 percent or more vocational majors nearly quadrupled.[1]

This shift calls into question the relevance of liberal arts education and whether the humanities could have a future. Could there be a place for literature, art, history, and philosophy in our universities and in a world dominated by vocational training, science, technology, and business? What is at stake with this current change for the university but also society and the future of humanity, politically, culturally, and existentially?

THE HUMANITIES AT RISK

According to Frank Donoghue, policymakers have cut budgets allocated to higher education in such a way that the center of gravity of universities has moved further away from the humanities. As public higher education ceased to promote civic responsibility and American colleges and universities went from being state supported to state located, the question at hand became not only whether the humanities could survive in the twenty-first century but also whether anyone should care about it.[2]

Alongside this academic reorientation was a sizable decrease in public funding for the humanities: "The National Science Foundation (NSF) grants went from being five times the size of their National Endowment for the Humanities (NEH) equivalents in 1979 to thirty-three times in 1997. In 2007, the NEH received 0.5 percent of the National Institute of Health's (NIH) budget and 3 percent of the NSF's, while in 2010, a pitiful 0.45 percent of federal research support went to the humanities."[3]

Pointing out that the humanities endowment's budget amounted to one-tenth of 1 percent of the federal government's total research and development budget, Jim Leach, the ninth chairman of the National Endowment for the Humanities, warned of a crisis in humanities research. Also commenting on this attrition, Cornell University president David Skorton argued in his 2010 State of the University address that it was time for university leaders to defend the humanities by articulating their significance.

The purpose of the present volume is to examine how the raison d'être and state of the humanities have academic but also cultural, political, societal, and existential ramifications. The humanities sharpen the human ability to think critically and differently; challenge assumptions, norms, and traditions; open citizens to the world; and provide an ethical dimension to people's thoughts and actions.

In order to explain the current trends putting the humanities' future at risk, we must first explore what caused them to be perceived as irrelevant and made vulnerable to policymakers. To some, this lack of public support originated from "academy-bashing" perpetrated by an ill-informed body of critics both within and outside universities who believe that, instead of teaching, scholars in the humanities devote their time and tax-dollar allocations to "useless" research. Others, including "humanists," attribute this decline to the introduction of new theoretical paradigms such as Marxism, poststructuralism, and feminism.

The implications of either diagnosis are, first, that humanities advocates have failed to make their case effectively; second, that too much emphasis has been placed in higher education on students' intellectual development rather than their preparedness for careers; third, that the humanities should abandon its liberal ambition and instead focus on seeking what its practical and economic values might be; and/or fourth, that the humanities should return to being what they were previously, when only a small number of the population attended college: a place for the privileged.

The call to abandon the tenets of liberal education and keep what would remain of it for the wealthy, as suggested above, raises fundamental issues about the role of education in a democratic society, and the responsibility of a city, state, or country in the education of its citizens. But assessing the real value and contribution of the humanities in the context of the marketization of higher education and the collapse of state funding in public education is, indeed, an essential task.

Arguments for and against the nonessential nature of the humanities have been raised by generations of scholars. Responding to an article by David Maxwell published in March 1968, Albert William Levi compellingly contended that the humanities had not become irrelevant. A professor of business economics at Indiana University, Maxwell had alleged that there existed a methodological gap between the humanities and their ostensible goals and that research in the field often lacked purpose and direction: "Since we do not know the process by which the goals of the humanities are furthered, we often cannot screen out those research efforts which make little or no contribution to this end from those that contribute significantly."[4]

Similar queries are raised today about the uncertainty surrounding the methodology and value of liberal education. First, what are or should be the aims of the humanities? Second, in the absence of quantitative assessment to adequately or scientifically measure their importance, how can one gauge the extent to which their goals or objectives are met? Many humanists today could share Levi's eloquent response:

> What I do think is valuable about current attacks upon the humanities is that they will prevent us from simply taking our work for granted [. . .] The humanities cannot be dismissed. Far from being outmoded, they are eternally relevant precisely because they are the arts of communication, the arts of continuity, and the arts of criticism. Language remains the indispensable medium within which we move and breathe. History provides that group memory which makes the communal bond possible. Philosophic criticism is the only activity through which man's self-reflection modifies the conditions of his existence. The cup of the humanities, therefore, must be the vessel from which we drink our life.[5]

Maxwell asked important questions: What are the goals of the humanities? How are they furthered, and how can we measure their contribution to the university or society? Levi's response—that the humanities are essential through the study of language, history, and/or philosophy—suggests that they serve a purpose beyond their intrinsic value, as they offer the means of modifying the conditions of human existence. In this respect, the humanities represent for Levi a dimension of higher education that we undermine at our own risk.

Revealing the dangers this undermining may entail for society is one of the aims of this book. In today's context, marked by the rise of postmodernism and posthumanism, Maxwell's interrogations and Levi's responses become all the more crucial to explore. Our first task will be to examine to what extent the objectives of liberal education are still possible or desirable to achieve. Second, we will consider how its importance should be examined from a pedagogical, political, and interdisciplinary perspective, and through a reconceptualization of the relation between the university and society.

DISCONNECTIONS: THEORY, SOCIETY, POLITICS

Traditional critics and policymakers often identify a gap between the humanities' theoretical writing and the need or interest of the public at large. They contend, for example, that the methodology of doctoral research and academic scholarship fails to engage with broad audiences on pertinent issues outside the university. They underscore the importance of knowing the intellectual legacy of past authors and thinkers and condemn the devaluation of the Great Books. According to Allan Bloom, the new impoverishment of liberal education is leading the American people to an intellectual predicament that he identifies as a civilizational crisis.

This perceived disconnect between scholars and nonacademics originated, for some conservatives, from a pedagogical failure of great magnitude driven by political correctness and the sweeping aside of values. Denying stable meanings and/or opening interpretation to "gamesmanship," poststructuralist theory allegedly introduced a form of circular incredulity and semantic nihilism.

In his presidential address at the 2004 MLA conference, Robert Scholes contended that the failure of theory represented "the larger failure of the humanities, as a whole, to justify their place in the academic world and the larger world as well."[6] Postmodernist and deconstructionist theories, as illustrated by Richard Klein, leave the academic world and specifically the liberal arts with great uncertainty about their very nature and existence:

> The future of literary criticism will be Derridean, or it will not be, and if it is not, it will have been Derridean, since it was he who first envisioned critically the possibility of a future from which literature—and, a fortiori, literary criticism—might be absent. Derrida noted that the exceptional fragility of literature would become manifest in the event of a nuclear, biological, or nanotechnological holocaust [. . .] Literature conforms to no referent from which it could be reconstituted if its canons were lost, the way chemistry might in a post-nuclear age be rediscovered. It depends for its existence exclusively on the preservation of the archive.[7]

On the one hand, Klein's argument—which alludes to the deconstruction of the metaphysics of presence—is valid from an anti-foundational perspective that highlights the absence of referent in literature and criticism. This approach constitutes de facto a challenge for the aspirations of liberal education to partake in the improvement of individuals and society.

But Klein's affirmation is also problematic because it does not seem to take into account the possibility of other theoretical approaches to reading literature. My aim is not to downplay the importance of the critic's contentions but to underscore both the significance and limits of theory—specifically how it can be wrongly perceived within and outside the academic world as a self-involved endeavor driven by abstraction, with a lack of attention to concrete societal issues.

On the other hand, Derrida has argued that ethics or the attainment of virtue could be conceivable in a deconstructionist or postmodernist world. Deconstruction is ethically important, and it does not necessarily have hyper-relativistic or nihilistic implications. It rests on the primacy of critical thinking:

> I am referring to the right to deconstruction as an unconditional right to ask critical questions not only to the history of the concept of man, but to the history even of the notion of critique, to the form and the authority of the question, to the interrogative form of thought. [. . .] The university should thus be the place in which nothing is beyond question. [8]

Shifting his attention from purely theoretical issues to the realm of human praxis, Derrida contends that "the university should remain the ultimate place of critical resistance." Such an "unconditional resistance" must oppose the university to state, economic, media, ideological, and cultural powers: "In short, all the powers that limit the democracy to come."[9] His questioning thus has pedagogical and political implications.

In accordance with Derrida, Henry Giroux critiqued the academics inhabiting a world populated by concepts, indifferent to broader public issues, and making no connections to audiences outside of the academy. Calling for a "critical pedagogy" through which students and faculty might respond to the demands of civic engagement, he condemned a form of theory that "degenerates into a performance for a small coterie of academics happily ensconced in a professionalized, gated community marked by linguistic privatization, indifference to translating private issues into public concerns, and a refusal to connect the acquisition of theoretical skills to the exercise of social power."[10]

In order to assess Giroux's argument, we must distinguish between the different theoretical paradigms he has in mind. It seems evident, for example, that Marxist or feminist studies are more socially rooted than anti-foundationalism and more likely to receive Giroux's support. It should also be observed that the nature of the "disconnect" between theory and concrete societal issues varies according to the different political and moral viewpoints of a commentator.

This is particularly true when one considers how many conservative voices find the inclusion of LGBT, Queer, or Middle Eastern issues to the curriculum too radical. They have held theory responsible for a breakdown in moral values and for failing to defend traditional approaches to philosophy, literature, and the arts.

However one reconciles postmodernism or deconstruction with the possibility or impossibility to reach the truth and/or lead to individual virtue, the fact that the humanities' research and theoretical outcomes find themselves at the center of the political debate is proof of their import within and beyond academia.

The 2012 American presidential election revealed this reality when Rick Santorum claimed that universities in the United States had become "indoctrination mills." The Republican candidate criticized colleges for teaching multiculturalism and environmentalism and for having an adversarial stance to American culture and Judeo-Christian religions. According to Santorum, this indoctrination was one of the keys to the Left holding and maintaining power and explained why Americans exaggerated the value of higher education.

Is literary theory responsible for the deprecation of the humanities, or has it fallen victim to the American tradition of anti-intellectualism? Whatever the answer to this question might be, its significance within and beyond the university cannot be denied.

The ongoing debate about liberal education and over the role of theory can also be seen as an opportunity to broaden and problematize the learning experience. Postmodern, posthuman, and deconstructionist theories in higher education promote critical thinking and intellectual debates, which are an essential component of education's vitality. Through them, students, researchers, and scholars question reality (or shed a different light on it). They critically examine the functioning of "indoctrination mills," whether their source is found in a viewpoint, a political party, or a university.

Questioning and rediscovering is at the core of what education should be, and exploring the construction of knowledge, or how epistemological norms determine thought, self, and society, lies at the heart of this process. Theory makes students—and future lawyers, teachers, and leaders alike—rethink what, why, and how they learn; it also leads those who teach to reexamine the extent to which the curricular choices they make as faculty impact the students' educational experience.

Theories also have their limits, however. An appreciation of the humanities cannot be limited to the knowledge and practice of theory. It also includes experiencing a broad range of works of literature, philosophy, art, and music: reading the classics, attending a play, listening to a symphony, studying a painting. These activities, which do not necessarily involve or demand a theoretic reflection, are equally essential to any higher educational experience.

In addition, teaching and learning should not be limited to theories or analyses, as important as they might be, for fear that, as Michel de Montaigne came to recognize in the late sixteenth century, it becomes more important to interpret the interpretations than to interpret the things. Noting that there were more books about books than about any other subject, he regretted that we did little but write glosses about each other. Beyond disseminating theory, teaching should henceforth be, according to him, about the discovery and understanding of primary sources.

All things considered, making the case for the humanities in today's world requires, as suggested by Derrida and Giroux, reconciling deconstruction and postmodernism with critical thinking; border-crossing; expanding debates and conversations; reconceiving the relation among education, ethics, and politics; and the link between the university and society.

Any initiator of this attempt (or essay, as Montaigne would put it) must face and seek to engage critically with the following challengers: first, those who rightly inquire like Maxwell about what the goals of the humanities are, and how they can be furthered and their contribution measured. Second, those for whom, like Stanley Fish, the humanities are their own good and should not serve any purpose other than being enjoyed for what they are.

Third, those who maintain that higher education should be primarily vocational and aim only at preparing students for their future profession. Fourth, those who believe that theory is too politically oriented and detrimental to the traditional aims of liberal education. And fifth, those who underscore the aporetic nature of an education that claims to make people or society better through the "invention of the other" and the assumption that knowledge necessarily leads to virtue.

Taking into account how critical thinking entails both a crisis and an opportunity to extend the boundaries of knowledge, we will examine these issues in a pluralistic more than systematic fashion by remaining attentive and intellectually receptive to the diversity of points of view. In that regard, we would comply with Terry Eagleton who, in *After Theory*, probed the limits of postmodernism and did not downplay the importance of continuing to ask the big questions.

THE LIMITS OF ANTI-FOUNDATIONALISM AND ANTI-HUMANISM

Beyond the instability of science, Matthew Arnold believed that humankind would discover that poetry and literature offered higher means to interpret life. Through the latter only, the uneducated English masses could be molded into conscientious individuals who strive for human perfection. The pursuit of culture, he argued, enabled any student to know the best that has been thought and said in the world.

However, the notion that liberal education could foster independent thinking, cultivate moral and intellectual virtue, lead to personal introspection, and promote social action was significantly tested by the emergence of different schools of academic thought during the decades that followed World War II.

Among these developments, structuralism approached works of literature as the result of impersonal forces, not human creation, in which the author as individual disappeared before a text's pattern, which had no subjective origin. According to this interpretation, so-called authors inhabited preexisting structures, enabling them to only convey the "already written." By erasing the author, structuralism represented a major challenge to the humanist tradition.

While classical humanism held that the human self was the source and measure of all things and the center of meaning, truth, and knowledge, structuralism saw in it an object of study whose identity and presence were no longer secure. Instead of being grounded, the self became provisional, relative, and socially constructed. In this context, language created rather than reflected reality, as well as the human ability to explain, comprehend, teach, and learn.

The emergence of structuralist approaches to literature, art, and culture challenged the legitimacy of the claims and aspirations of liberal education and the humanities to emancipate the subject. Following Saussure, who viewed language as a system of signs that preceded subjectivity, Barthes foregrounded his semiological work with the proclamation of the dissolution of the individual subject.

Furthermore, with deconstruction, Derrida challenged all philosophical systems that presumed a center such as being, essence, or truth, and attempted to explain the relations between the self and the world. Because every system posited a center or presence, Derrida pointed to structuralism as the "moment" when philosophers were able to see their systems not as absolute truth, but as constructs or structures. Since what was assembled could be changed, put into play, destabilized, or altered, the self or the idea of "being human" that was also conceptualized from and within language could also be deconstructed. It was an illusion produced by language's impersonal structure.

From an anti-foundationalist perspective, Stanley Fish's contentions about the humanities can be interpreted in light of nihilistic and hyper-relativistic postures. First, Fish argued that the humanities were of no pragmatic value: "To the question of what use are the humanities? The only honest answer is none whatsoever." Second, a justification for the humanities conferred "value on an activity from a perspective outside its performance" and thus implied the presence of a thinking subject. Third, Fish opposed the view that the humanities should aim at making humans more noble or virtuous: "An activity that cannot be justified is an activity that refuses to regard itself as instrumental to some larger good. The humanities are their own good."[11]

Fish's anti-foundationalist stance logically rejected the pragmatic subordination of knowledge to practical action. It dismissed essentialism and cast a doubt on the necessity of and justification for any intellectual or ethical inquiry. As such, he put in question not only the foundations and use of knowledge but also the goals of liberal education.

Fish opposed totalizing visions of social, scientific, or historical reality and affirmed the contingent nature of human beliefs. At best, his stance was relativistic and contradictory. As Terry Eagleton argued: "Like almost all diatribes against universalism, Fish's critique of universalism has its own rigid universals: the priority at all times and places of sectoral interests, the permanence of conflict, the a priori status of belief systems, the rhetorical character of truth, the fact that all apparent openness is secretly closure, and the like."[12]

At worst, Fish's theoretical views resulted in extreme relativism and radical subjectivism. According to David Hirsch, the critic wandered "in his own Elysian fields, hopelessly alienated from art, from truth, and from humanity."[13]

Both anti-humanistic and anti-foundationalist theories challenge the principles of the humanities that upheld the belief that education can be a guide toward emancipation from ignorance or tyranny. Perhaps the most formidable proponent of anti-humanism, Friedrich Nietzsche argued that the idealistic vision of emancipation through education was meant to constrain the strong for the benefit of the weak and that it thus denied the unrestrained Dionysian forces of life rather than fostering them.

Nietzsche's allegation revealed the unavoidable association between knowledge and power and the aporetic dimension of education. A contentious issue regarding the relevance of the humanities concerns the question of "humanism," a naïve anthropomorphism grounded in metaphysics for Heidegger.

Contrary to Fish, however, it is important to note that Derrida contended that abandoning the myth of foundations did not lead to nihilism. He acknowledged that "a total rupture with the metaphysical tradition of philosophy [was] impossible. We always already inhabit the 'inside' of the metaphysical tradition [. . .]. The main reason for the deconstruction of metaphysics [being] explicitly ethical and political [. . .] Derrida does not hand us in antifoundationalism."[14]

The question of the foundation of humanism and being human is key to appreciating the possibilities of liberal education, for it can be argued that belief, reason, logic, or argumentation need foundation. Derrida's humanism in this respect does not entail a reflection about what humans are or ought to be, but a continued inquiry that dismantles preconceived understandings and seeks to recognize difference and the alterity of the other.

Beyond anti-humanism and anti-foundationalism, this study not only takes into account but also follows the idea according to which students' emancipation after deconstruction calls for an interdisciplinary pedagogy that involves decentering, remapping, and reterritorializing. It also contends that this radical approach, which brings to light the ethical and political dimension of education, is most essentially revealed in the realm of the humanities.

THE END OF DEMOCRACY?

Inscribed in history, the realm of education encompasses the ethical and political domains. More specifically, the well-being of democracy was from its inception associated with the development of the humanities that promoted the attainment of moral and intellectual virtue and the search for the common good.

Francis Fukuyama's prediction—that the fall of Communism and the end of the Cold War brought forth the end of history and that the "universalization" of democracy and peace among nations would follow—did not fully grasp the challenges to come in the twenty-first century: not only the struggle among peoples of diverse cultural and religious backgrounds, but also, from an environmental standpoint, the conflict between planet Earth and civilization that no human being is assured to survive.

How does true democracy take root and not fall into an oligarchic and despotic form of authority? How do we put an end to the death of eighteen million people a year in the world from hunger and preventable diseases? How do we address the root causes of the conflict in the Middle East, confront terrorism, and give back to politics its *lettres de noblesse* by making it the realm of the possible?

For Tocqueville, America provided a model from which one could study the functioning of a democratic form of government. In an 1850 prefatory note to the twelfth edition of *Democracy in America*, he contended that the fundamental principles of the American Constitution (order, balance of powers, true liberty, and the sincere respect for the law) were indispensable to all republics. They had to be known to all, and where they would not be met, the republic would soon cease to exist.

The spirit of Tocqueville's writing extended to Dwight Eisenhower's final public address, which warned that the abuse of power could endanger the survival of American democracy. The late president famously warned his television audience against the acquisition of unwarranted influence by the military-industrial complex and the potential for the disastrous rise of misplaced power that would endanger the preservation of the American people's liberties or democratic processes. John F. Kennedy's predecessor underscored the role and responsibility of each individual in a society led by materialism and short-sighted chronic consumerism:

> Only an alert and knowledgeable citizenry [could] avoid the impulse to live only for today, plundering for our own ease and convenience the precious resources of tomorrow. We cannot mortgage the material assets of our grand-

children without risking the loss also of their political and spiritual heritage. We want democracy to survive for all generations to come, not to become the insolvent phantom of tomorrow.[15]

Modern democracy had already been tested, its vulnerability and near collapse manifest in the earlier part of the twentieth century. Published in 1919, Paul Valéry's "The Crisis of the Mind" underlined the mortality of later civilizations in the aftermath of the massive death and destruction caused by World War I: "We see now that the abyss of history is deep enough to hold us all. We are aware that a civilization has the same fragility as a life."[16]

More importantly, World War I highlighted the danger of technological progress, the limits of static knowledge and unchallenged systems of values, the rise of suspicion, and the collapse of ideals: "So many horrors could not have been possible without so many virtues. Doubtless, much science was needed to kill so many, to waste so much property, and annihilate so many cities in so short a time; but *moral qualities* in like number were also needed."[17]

The military crisis of World War I set in motion an intellectual crisis. Following the deaths of thousands of young writers and artists, the illusion of a European culture had been lost; according to Valéry, knowledge had proved impotent to save anything. Science was mortally wounded in its mortal ambitions, and, as it were, put to shame by the cruelty of its applications.

The outcome of the war demonstrated that the fate of a civilization could not rest solely on scientific and technological achievement, or the illusion of laissez-faire economics that would lead ten years later to the most dramatic global crisis. Ultimately, both were important factors that contributed to the rise of fascism, Nazi death camps, the death of fifty million people worldwide, and a series of crimes against humanity whose brutality the world had never known.

The horrific outcomes of the two world wars, fought among so-called cultured and civilized nations, brought forth a disillusionment that has carried over into the postmodern age. In his *Wartime Writings*, Antoine de Saint-Exupéry lamented humanity's descent into a dark abyss and the loss of the ideals that inspire us to act in service to something greater than ourselves.

This sentiment was later echoed by Theodor Adorno, who bemoaned that poetry would no longer be possible after Auschwitz. In the heart of European culture, it was argued that humanism proved powerless in the face of Nazism's depravity: "In the personal lives of the butchers and torturers, a cultivated literacy, a taste for music and the arts can be documented. One can play and sing Schubert in the evening and torture in the morning."[18]

These testimonies cast a doubt on the humanities' capacity to confront and help alleviate the major crises of the modern world marked by violence and horrific destruction. They also defy humanism's credo put forth by Pico della Mirandola that the study of the arts and Classics would temper the "human animal" in each of us.

Nonetheless, Adorno and Steiner missed the mark in holding poetry and music to account for being incapable, or worse, seemingly complicit in the crimes committed against humanity. Was art responsible for the death of millions and the destruction of life, or was it rather caused by the perversion of its interpreters? What truths did art unveil that dictatorial regimes were pressed to hide or distort?

The 2013 film *The Monuments Men*, directed by George Clooney, reveals art as a cultural heritage worthy of preservation, but it also questions the diverse significances that masterpieces and the humanities in general could have in different political contexts. For the Nazis and its followers, art's preservation or destruction was based on self-glorification and gratification of conquerors and their exploitation of other cultures. Conversely, for the soldiers of democracy (despite the imperfections of its system), art inspired a sense of elevation and respect for diverse expressions of beauty that transcended all human difference.

Contemplating these queries in light of Adorno's and Steiner's comments, it is revealing that the totalitarianisms of the twentieth century, and current forms of despotic regimes or terrorist organizations such as North Korea, ISIS, or any around the world, are opposed in theory and practice to all the major tenets and values of liberal education: broadening critical thinking; continuously reexamining the ends of ethics and moral philosophy; respecting diversity of opinions and embracing pluralism; and questioning truth and common knowledge. Without these democratic principles being actively sought in our universities, free institutions and personal liberty would inevitably be imperiled.

We will seek to shed a new light in this respect on the political and democratic dimension of a pedagogy that invites students to read and write differently, deconstruct knowledge, and rehabilitate the other, whether individuals or points of view. The humanities are central to this process. They lead students to explore counterdiscourses and question received assumptions. They provide the means to think independently in order to make choices and to participate in the life of their academic institutions and beyond.

The link between the humanities and democracy becomes all the more real when one considers that the creation of the State Humanities Council and the National Endowment for the Humanities took place during eras that saw the advancement of democratic principles. The implementations of the New Deal and the Great Society were political programs that aimed to alleviate the crisis of the Great Depression and the grave injustice of segregation. These correlations reinforce the view that democracy cannot exist without educated citizens.

In the same vein, art, music, and literature give students the capacity to uncover new frames of reference and correspondence between self and the world, and to work toward a collective destiny across different societies. Discovering other cultures; uncovering their past, norms, and traditions; learning new languages—all are ways through which the humanities extend the boundaries of our self-awareness and broaden our understanding of the world anthropologically, existentially, and spiritually.

Why, one might ask, should we acquire these new forms of knowledge, and toward what aims? It is in order to extend ourselves toward others and "the other" within ourselves via our individual and collective struggle for meaning, justice, peace, and democracy. Many examples around the world demonstrate how censorship of scholarship and the arts correlate with political oppression. Asked about the decreasing support of the humanities in her host country of the United States, the challenges faced by many liberal arts colleges, and the proposed cuts to arts and literature programs, Azar Nafisi, author of *Reading Lolita in Tehran*, contended that the decline of the humanities would lead to a lessening of our humanity.

PEDAGOGICAL AND INTERDISCIPLINARY PERSPECTIVES

The current study does not systematically reject but questions and challenges comprehensive visions of social, scientific, or historical reality; in short, it contends that the case for the humanities can be made more effectively from an interdisciplinary point of view. Particular attention will be paid to the fields of economics and STEM, whose academic prestige is on the rise and yet remains unchallenged, contrary to that of the humanities. [19]

It is striking that important questions remain unanswered concerning both fields' raison d'être: how are the goals of economics, science, and technology furthered and their contributions measured? To what extent do they uphold the principles of emancipation and equality, and do they recognize education's role in bettering society?

As important as they have become within and outside the ivory tower, they differ significantly from the sphere of the humanities. While the latter addresses questions of value, what is right or wrong, or what ought to be done, economics, science, and technology are generally more concerned with matters of fact and data based on empirical evidence.

Raising concerns for the life of others through narrative imagination and focusing on thinking critically about questions of value, liberal education gives students the means to cross boundaries and question the paths taken by science, whether social or physical, from an ethical perspective. Unlike technology, it provides individuals with the ability to problematize teaching and research in the scientific disciplines through a humanistic perspective of which positive science (which does not go beyond what is evident from the observation or experimentation) is deprived.

Through the humanities (e.g., reading literary or philosophical texts and writing from a broad range of cultural and social settings), students inquire about what is good and what ought to be, beyond what "factually" exists. Without them, the fields of economics and STEM run the risk of being stripped of ethical criticism and judgment, and are cut off from the reality of human experience.

In this respect, our aim will be to demonstrate how literature, philosophy, and critical theory enable students to explore and question, like the feminist economist Julie A. Nelson questions, the justification of neoliberal economics' models and methodology, or Hans Jonas, the ultimate aim of science and technology.

The study of the humanities reveals the extent to which economics, science, or technology result from discourses that are not value-free. Differing from the view that teaching and research in economics and STEM are only based on facts, we contend that they ensue from rhetorical constructions that are never neutral. They originate from and lead to decisions motivated by value that in turn influence choices about what hypotheses to discard or pursue that may impact society.

The humanities envisaged here contradict the "anti-humanism" manifest in positive economics, scientism, and technology. In the area of economics, Louis Althusser referred to anti-humanism to contend that all impersonal forms of socioeconomic power had primacy over the subject. The human individual, he argued, was only the product of social practices. Althusser thus downplayed the role of human agency in the process of history.

One can draw a parallel in this respect between Althusser's anti-humanism and laissez-faire capitalism, both of which, in spite of their different implications, downplay the primacy of individuals in society.

From a pedagogical perspective, John Maynard Keynes critiqued the abstract and dehumanized forms of positive economics in capitalist societies that resulted in "concoctions, as imprecise as the initial assumptions they rest on [and] which allow[ed] the author to lose sight of the complexities and interdependencies of the real world in a maze of pretentious and unhelpful symbols."[20]

Like positive economics, which assumes to be value-free and whose purpose is to investigate "what is" rather than "what ought to be," science and technology also bear within themselves the danger of anti-humanism. Positivism already stressed in the nineteenth century that data derived from experience and mathematical treatments constituted the exclusive source of authoritative knowledge in the social and natural sciences.

Indeed, positivism was marked by the ultimate position that science resulting from facts and experiments provided the only valid form of knowledge whatsoever. Rejecting introspective and intuitive understanding, only "positive" science, according to Auguste Comte, could provide an explanation for a humanity abandoned in an indifferent universe. Alexander Rosenberg recently reaffirmed the notion that science could be the only reliable source of knowledge.[21]

Seeking to challenge the dogmatic endorsement of scientific methodology and the reduction of all knowledge to what is measurable, Tzvetan Todorov criticized trends of thought that emphasized science and tended toward a deterministic view of the world: "Scientism decides that since the results of science are valid for everyone, this must be something shared, not individual. In practice, the individual must submit to the collectivity, which 'knows' better than he does." Historically contextualizing these developments, he also noted that "the first variant of scientism was put into practice by totalitarian regimes."[22]

Similarly, scientism, positive economics, or STEM open the door to a form of post-humanism in which no essential differences or absolute demarcations can be made between bodily existence and computer simulation, cybernetic mechanism and biological organism, robot teleology and human aspirations: "Human technologies have produced a hyper-complex environment for which humanist distinction between the moral, the human, and the technological are increasingly non-functional."[23] The role of the humanities is crucial in this respect to seek a redefinition of what it means to be human.

AFTER THE POSTMODERN/POSTHUMAN?

What can be the place of the humanities in a postmodern era marked by the rise and decisive influence of business, economics, and STEM in our universities? Jean-François Lyotard contended that knowledge formation had been altered in our postindustrial era. The information age, he argued, affected the circulation of learning, and anything that was not translatable technologically would be abandoned.

Furthermore, as the suppliers and users of knowledge became commodity producers and consumers, the distribution of informational goods and the mercantilization of education took on, according to Lyotard, a political significance: "Knowledge and power are simply two sides of the same question: who decides what knowledge is, and who knows what needs to be decided? In the computer age, the question of knowledge is now more than ever a question of government."[24]

In the context described above and the one that sees a drastic decline of public funding in higher education, the role of educators in the humanities is to recognize and cross "the epistemological, political, cultural, and social margins that structure the language of history, power and difference [and] create pedagogical conditions in which students become border crossers in order to understand otherness in its own terms."[25]

Recognizing the workings of power in society toward specific ends, it becomes urgent for students and academics to continue to think and write critically, to situate themselves in history, and to question and transgress the established boundaries of knowledge.

The assimilation and transmission of knowledge in our postmodern age should thus not be isolated from political considerations. No clear boundary exists between the ivory tower and the outside world. Beyond the positive nature of physical or social science ("what is"), the humanities expand one's intellectual inquiry to examine "what ought to be." They bear an emancipatory potential that naturally generates individual and societal change through independent thinking and critical awareness—a potential to reconnect the text and the world, the academic discipline and the cultural process; to recognize the link between power and truth; and to expose students to difference and otherness.

In short, the humanities provide students and faculty—and all citizens of the world—with the ability to struggle against any form of power that seeks to transform them into objects or instruments in the sphere of knowledge, truth, consciousness, and discourse.

Putting one's intellect in the service of a more democratic society demands a critical investigation of current positive economic, scientific, and technological learning. By interrogating where ideology, power, and knowledge converge in these fields of study, one foresees a postmodern approach in which the questions of virtue, ethics, and the good precede those of knowledge and truth. Beyond foundationalist and essentialist myths, the "death" of philosophy and ethics does not entail, according to Zygmunt Bauman, the dissolution of the moral.

We emphasize here the multifaceted nature of the postmodern that on the one hand challenges objective knowledge, totalities, universal values, and grand historical narratives while still considering ethical concerns, and, on the other hand, one that gives preeminence to play over purpose and aporia over interpretation.

The concepts of rhizome, micronarratives, or deconstruction, for example, do not necessarily preclude a moral dimension and ethics of responsibility from academic research; they rather enable the scholar to reconceptualize moral and ethical needs, norms, and values.

This reconceptualization can only be achieved through the realms of the humanities that for this reason, among others, need to be brought back to the center of academic life. The political and pedagogical implications of this interdisciplinary study thus entail a renewed criticism of the relation between higher education, society, and the world at large (politically, economically, scientifically, and technologically) and the importance of the humanities within it.

THE CASE FOR THE HUMANITIES

The premise of this book is based on the notion that we live in a time of crisis: our technologically driven world possesses the means of its own destruction; economic and financial policies undermine the very existence of our democracy; and the postmodern, posthuman age fundamentally challenges our ability and legitimacy to conceive future ideals.

In the midst of this scientific, economic, political, environmental, and existential crisis, the humanities need to be valued at the level of their eminent importance. They constitute an essential path through which citizens need to reflect about the meaning of their lives from an existential point of view, but also interrogate how they should live, from ethical, social, and political perspectives.

Furthermore, the humanities represent an indispensable means through which students must explore the purpose and telos of their education and what their role in society can be in light of the formidable challenges humanity faces today. They must measure, in the postmodern context, the challenge and responsibility to conceive and partake in full conscience in the transformation of society toward greater justice and democracy.

Toward this end, the present volume seeks to respond to the following questions: How are the humanities useful, and what purpose do they serve? Why is the space devoted to literature, art, history, and/or philosophy in our universities critical in a world dominated by science, technology, and economics? Why do we educate, and what end do we assign the humanities through this process? How are the humanities connected to the challenges of society and conducive to creating a more democratic world? What is the real worth and function of the humanities compared to and in conjunction with other fields of study and research such as economics and STEM?

The breadth of this project calls for a reflection that is interdisciplinary. More than any other academic field, the humanities inspire students to explore the relation between the university and society, knowledge and power, and to develop their capacity for synthesis, critical thinking, ethical vocation, and civic participation. They are essential and far more valuable than business, economics, science, or technology because they lead us to not only question the world as it is but also how it ought to be.

Chapter 1 (The Humanities in the City) demonstrates how this latter inquiry has been at the heart of liberal arts education since antiquity. It situates epistemologically how current issues pertaining to the humanities' aim and value (e.g., their purpose and relevance in society, the role of public education funding, the formation of future citizens, the search for the common good) have been debated through modern times.

Ancient authors and philosophers interrogate the why, how, and purpose of human existence through their reflections on the essential role of higher education to promote civic responsibility and conceive of a better world. Their works constitute in this respect a model through which the teaching and interpretation of economics and STEM must be reenvisioned today. At stake with this reconceptualization, which calls for border-crossing and a rehabilitation of the other through critical pedagogy, is the extent to which humanity can or should be in control of its destiny.

Building from Clark Kerr's reflection on the social and societal benefits of the humanities, chapter 2 (Humanizing Economics) argues, first, that the study of economics is enhanced by a human-centered approach to teaching and interpreting the discipline through the study of its rhetoric (McCloskey) and sociohistorical reality (Mirowski); second, that literary narratives (e.g., Steinbeck) reveal the gap between economic theories based on mechanistic and mathematized determinism and actual socioeconomic experience; third, how the humanities challenge the tenets of mainstream economics through renewed perspectives on *homo economicus* (Bourdieu), "libidinal economy" (Lyotard), and critical pedagogy (Giroux); and fourth, that feminist economics expose both the fate of minorities and subalterns in the developing world.

Chapter 3 (Searching for STEM's *telos*) argues that the role of the humanities is fundamental to define the limits, ends, and/or purpose of science and technology (what is versus ought to be). We discuss, first, how poetry, music, and philosophy enable scientists to think more broadly and creatively, and also reveal aspects of nature and reality that are not accessible via scientific methods (e.g., Da Vinci, Einstein); second, how the exploration of fictional and historical narratives is essential in considering the neutral or nonneutral nature of technology and its impact on society and the common good (Jonas); and third, how in contrast to scientific and materialistic determinism, the humanities are needed to set moral boundaries to the development of modern technologies, transhumanism, and posthumanism.

In contrast with postmodern and posthuman absolutes, and beyond the limits of the individual's presence, chapter 4 (Transcendent Humanities) focuses on how the humanities move students beyond themselves toward a renewed collective consciousness and responsibility: first, through the three stages of bibliotherapy (identification, catharsis, and insight) in war, genocide, and Holocaust literature; second, through the crossing of subjective and cultural boundaries illustrated in Said's conception of counterpoint; and third—beyond the limits of positive science, vocational training, and the marketization of education—through the humanities' enabling us to be inspired and engaged artistically, politically, cross-culturally, and existentially on issues pertaining to the present and future of the human condition and its environment.

The defense of the humanities envisioned in this book involves close analysis, theoretical considerations, and the search for a renewed relation between higher education and society. The humanities must respond to the urgent need for students to explore their fields of academic inquiry from broader political, socioeconomic, technological, and existential perspectives. Their level of consciousness must be raised and oriented toward the collective ideal of the common good. Only such crossing of academic, critical, and cultural boundaries can enhance our ability to think critically and form competent leaders both now and in the future.

NOTES

1. Victor E. Ferrall, *Liberal Arts at the Brink* (Cambridge: Harvard University Press, 2011), 3–4. The terms *liberal arts* and *humanities* are used interchangeably in this text. They primarily refer to the fields of literature, the arts, and philosophy.

2. Frank Donoghue, "Can the Humanities Survive the 21st Century?" *Chronicle of Higher Education*, September 5, 2010.

3. Toby Miller, *Blow Up the Humanities* (Philadelphia: Temple University Press, 2012), 12.

4. Albert William Levi, *The Humanities Today* (Bloomington: Indiana University Press, 1970), 92.

5. Levi, *The Humanities Today*, 92–93.

6. Robert Scholes, "Presidential Address 2004: The Humanities in a Posthumanist World," *PMLA* 120, no. 3 (2005): 730.

7. Richard Klein, "The Future of Literary Criticism," *PMLA* 125, no. 4 (2010): 920.

8. Jacques Derrida, "The Future of the Profession or the University without Condition (Thanks to the 'Humanities,' What *Could Take Place* Tomorrow," in Peter Pericles Trifonas and Michael A. Peters, eds. *Deconstructing Derrida: Tasks for the New Humanities* (New York: Palgrave Macmillan, 2005), 13.

9. Derrida, "The Future of the Profession or the University without Condition," 13.

10. Henry Giroux, "The Attack on Higher Education and the Necessity of Critical Pedagogy," in Sheila L. Macrine, ed. *Critical Pedagogy in Uncertain Times: Hope and Possibilities* (New York: Palgrave, 2009), 12.

11. Stanley Fish, "Will the Humanities Save Us?" Opinionator, *New York Times*, January 6, 2008.

12. Stanley Fish, "Review of *The Trouble with Principle* ," *London Review of Books* 22, no. 5 (2000): 10.

13. David Hirsch, *The Deconstruction of Literature: Criticism after Auschwitz* (Hanover, NH: Brown University Press, 1991), 68.

14. Michael A. Peters and Gert Biesta, *Derrida, Deconstruction, and the Politics of Pedagogy* (New York: Peter Lang, 2009), 30, 34.

15. Dwight Eisenhower, "Farewell Address to the Nation," January 17, 1961.

16. James R. Lawler, ed., *Paul Valéry: An Anthology* (Princeton, NJ: Princeton University Press, 1977), 94.

17. Lawler, *Paul Valéry*, 95.

18. Scholes, "Presidential Address 2004," 724–25.

19. The acronym STEM mainly refers in this study to science and technology.

20.   John Maynard Keynes, *The General Theory of Employment , Interest and Money* (Cambridge: MacMillan, 1936), 297.

21.   Alex Rosenberg, *The Atheist's Guide to Reality* (New York: W. W. Norton and Company, 2012).

22.   Tzvetan Todorov, *The Imperfect Garden* (Princeton, NJ: Princeton University Press, 2002), 23.

23.   Bruce Clarke, *Posthuman Metamorphosis: Narrative and Systems* (New York: Fordham University Press, 2008), 195.

24. Jean-François Lyotard, *The Postmodern Condition: A Report on Knowledge*, translated by Geoff Bennington and Brian Massumi (Minneapolis: University of Minnesota Press, 1984), 8–9.

25. Henry Giroux, *Border Crossings: Cultural Workers and the Politics of Education* (London: Routledge, 2005), 28–29.

Chapter One

The Humanities in the City

The lesser importance granted to the humanities in higher education represents a challenge for our universities and societies. This is particularly true when one considers the relation among higher education, democracy, and civic responsibility. Martha Nussbaum recently demonstrated that as "the humanities and the arts are being cut away [. . .] the future of the world's democracy hangs in the balance."[1]

The weakening of liberal education's importance, including literature, philosophy, and history, is detrimental to preparing students and future citizens to reflect on how they should live in the City, and face the political, technological, and existential challenges of our times.

The decrease in public funding for the humanities over the past decades has corresponded with the rise of democracy's crisis. Never have so many people been disillusioned by and disconnected with the political process. Never has money played such an important role in politics. Never has the financial situation of the country been in such dire condition: $20 trillion in debt and no solution in sight. Never has such a large number of people (forty-seven million) been living in poverty in the United States.

Through fostering critical thinking, moral and intellectual virtue, and cross-cultural awareness, the humanities impact the sociopolitical discursive formation. They are meant to fulfill a purpose and not simply be an end in themselves as Stanley Fish alleged. We must first consider where the ideals of modern democracy were born in order to understand the primary role authors and philosophers have played in their conceptions.

POLITY AND PEDAGOGY: BEYOND RELATIVITY

The debate about the humanities and its political significance was not born yesterday. Since antiquity, philosophers have explored the acquisition of moral and intellectual virtue, the role of the State in universities, and the pros and cons of liberal and professional education. They have also discussed whether education should be only an end in itself or aim at promoting critical thinking and civic responsibility.

The search for the common good through education was at the heart of Aristotle's *Nicomachean Ethics*. The Greek philosopher studied how living well among mortals was inseparable from attaining virtue (*arete*) and human happiness (*eudaimonia*). He did so, according to Robert C. Bartlett and Susan D. Collins, with the knowledge that being and doing good were relative entities: "Aristotle proceeds in full awareness of a version of relativism more radical and perhaps more impressive than our own."[2]

It is worth mentioning that the role of higher education in the City was already challenged by the uncertain understanding of what humans could or should achieve through it. Acquired knowledge did not necessarily result in goodness or virtue, or a clear understanding of how to measure and achieve the latter.

For the Sophist Protagoras, the idea that human beings were the measure of things meant that reality, judgment, and "truth" were dependent on an individual's perception, which could never be objective. The subjectivity of the physical realm applied also to that of the abstract—including what one held to be just or unjust, good or depraved. According to this relativist perspective, moral convictions resulted from transitory opinions.

The lesson for us is that the obstacles we face in our postmodern world today, comparable in some measures to the ones faced by Greek authors, ought not to steer us necessarily to Nietzsche's or Fish's line of reasoning. Aristotle's familiarity with contingency "did not lead him to abandon his inquiry into the human good. [Similarly,] our relativism [should not] grant us the license to forgo such an inquiry for ourselves."[3] In spite of the fragility of reason that he recognized, Aristotle supported the idea that *finis ultimus* (utmost aim) and *summum bonum* (greatest good) should be sought through education.

Socrates also faced the challenges of his opponents' contingent thinking when he argued that one could achieve *eudaimonia* (living well and happiness) by cultivating *arete* (virtue) through temperance and self-discipline. His belief that life was not worth living without seeking *eudaimonia* and *arete* was contested by the Sophist Thrasymachus, who contended that happiness could be equally gained by "behaving immorally instead of virtuously,"[4] and that justice only favored the interests of the stronger party.

Rejecting the Sophists' relativism, Socrates disputed the situational ethics proponents who claimed that moral principles were relative to a given period, locale, or circumstance. This opposition had major implications in the field of education that still reverberate today. While the Sophists endorsed only the utilitarian value of vocational and professional training, Socrates promoted a form of teaching and learning that cultivated the notion that all citizens needed to foster an ethical predisposition.

Like his mentor Socrates, Plato objected to the Sophists' claims. If opinion or belief dealt with context and what was changeable, knowledge encompassed in his view what was unchanging or eternal. Since it was immaterial, an abstract form or *eidos*, the task of education was to free individuals from their ignorance. In the allegory of the cave, Plato described human beings as prisoners who saw the world through a projection of distorted images that they perceived as reality. One only experienced true knowledge when one escaped this cave of sensation to discover the intelligible world in the realm of Ideas.

The aim of education, according to Plato, was to be elevated to the reality that lay beyond the phenomenal world: "The stars that decorate the sky [. . .] are far inferior [. . .] to the true realities; that is, to the true relative velocities, in pure numbers and perfect figures, of the orbits and what they carry with them, which are perceptible to reason and thought but not visible to the eye."[5]

The notion that human beings needed to free themselves from the bonds of their obliviousness revealed the fundamental relation that existed between the pedagogical, philosophical, and political spheres: "The society we have described can never grow into a reality or see the light of day, and there will be no ends to the troubles of states, or indeed, of humanity itself, until philosophers become kings in this world, or those we now call kings and rulers really and truly become philosophers."[6]

As familiar with the Sophists' relativism as Aristotle and Socrates, Plato did not abandon his search for the common good and the role education could play in this respect. One could not educate without a *telos*, an end that was both metaphysical and ethical. Plato's aim was to transform the Athenian political regime and make possible the instituting of democracy and justice in the City. Toward this political ambition, the public sphere was responsible for consolidating a system of education that produced citizens of good character.

Education was central to the functioning of the State. It had ethical and political ramifications. It called for a reconsideration of what existed beyond the perceived reality, an inquiry not only about the world as it was but as it could be.

In its historical and societal context, Plato intended through his vision of liberal education to put an end to the process of disintegration that was affecting Athens following the trial and suicide of Socrates. How could representatives concerned with justice and the well-being of its citizens have condemned the philosopher to death? Beyond contingency and relativity, Plato considered that the lover of wisdom was best suited to become the ideal political leader of a democratic society.

PUBLIC SCHOOL, MUSIC, AND CITIZENSHIP

From antiquity, the political implications of education revealed that if it was necessary for citizens to be virtuous, it was equally essential for the City to form righteous leaders. Through this individual-collective dialectic, Plato envisioned a correspondence between self and society, microcosm and macrocosm, contending that there existed parallels between the character of citizens and the State.

Each individual could be virtuous regardless of their status and position in society. The artisans could remedy their concupiscence (*epithumia*) through the virtue of temperance. Driven by emotion and desire (*thumos*), the warrior could find solace in the virtue of courage. Finally, the ruling political class could transform its intellectual capacity (*nous*) into the virtue of wisdom.

These symmetric relations underscored how education inspired individuals to live virtuous lives, and how justice was relative to the integrity of its leaders and citizens. Plato demonstrated that if the City resulted from what its citizens made of it, the citizens were in return what the City enabled them to be.

It is revealing that art played an essential role in this context. Specifically, a proper instruction in laws and politics demanded that students and future citizens be musically educated. Like the Pythagoreans, Plato stressed the cathartic function of music that poised the mind and expelled the passions troubling it.

Musical education took on a therapeutic function. It nurtured the soul toward the virtue of understanding and compassion. Works of art influenced students for good and led them into close sympathy and conformity with beauty and reason. Rhythm and harmony penetrated into the mind and took a most powerful hold providing grace and beauty.

It is also telling that in contrast with our current times in which music education has been pushed to the margin of higher education, the Latin *musica* and Greek *mousike* referred in antiquity to *musigena*, born of the muses that presided over the arts, and to the *mousikôs anèr*. The latter was seen as not only a musician or composer but also a cultivated and lettered individual who embodied the ideal expression of the educated Athenian citizen.

Sheramy D. Bundrick demonstrated the impact of music pedagogy on polity when she underscored that the "representations of youths receiving training in *mousike* that first appear in Athenian iconography [. . .] coincided with the rise of democracy and possibly the advents of schools in the city."[7] Music favored the emancipation of students as free and independent thinkers. Students acquired through it skills that enhanced their moral character.

Similarly, in contrast with today's dramatic reduction of State budgets allocated to higher education, Plato and Aristotle touted the importance of public schooling and the responsibility of the State in properly educating its citizens. They highlighted the insufficiencies of vocational training and would have opposed the humanities' current displacement away from the center of gravity of universities.

Like Plato, Aristotle rejected professional education contending that the activity of the mind should be freed from all material constraints. Beyond attaining skills necessary for professional development, the aim of education (etymologically *e-ducere*, "to bring out or develop a reality latent within us") was to awaken and orient the mind toward the practice of justice and the promotion of civic responsibility. In this respect, liberal arts and musical training instilled future leaders and citizens with the ability to distinguish vices from virtues.

Further, founded on his teleological conception of an orderly universe, Aristotle favored public education that he deemed too important to be left in the hands of private administrators. He considered that the availability of public schools, open to all, would increase the participation of citizens in the exercise of power.

We see a clear conflict between current trends in higher education and the philosophical underpinnings of effective democracy. Public schooling trained citizens for life beyond vocational purposes, and a City's excellence was based on its citizens' wisdom. Thus, virtue and the art of living individually and collectively needed to be learned. Aristotle also used a musical metaphor to underscore this idea: "Human beings consider the causes of happiness to be those good things that are external, as if the lyre rather than the art were to be held the cause of brilliant and beautiful lyre playing."[8]

The purpose of teaching and learning encompassed a political function as instruction sought to create the conditions necessary for the formation and unity of citizens. Representing a multitude, the City should be made one through education. Creating a virtuous polis contributed to the stability of a more democratic governance. For this reason, schooling ought to be the primary task of the legislator. Aristotle subscribed to the view that the ultimate responsibility for instruction lay in the public arena.

Through public schooling, the humanities were thus called to contribute to the democratization process of society. The latter must be considered here in its historical context since women, workers, and slaves were excluded from it. It is worth noting, however, that Plato and Aristotle envisioned through a public and liberal education the correlation between the individual and the collective, the future role of citizenry, and how one could learn to live well and contribute to society. In this respect, philosophy and music education supplied the elements that were lacking in nature.

Beyond Plato's abstract world of forms and ideas, Aristotle apprehended the role of education through the control over one's instincts and desires and the avoidance of deficit and excess. Moral and intellectual virtues enabled students to find a balance, a path between extremes. Attained through education, virtue constituted for Aristotle "the end [aim] of political life."[9] Public schooling and the study of music made possible in this respect the collective fulfillment of society through the promotion of the common good.

SENECA AND THE NECESSITY OF VIRTUE

We have seen how the well-being of democracy was from its inception associated with the development of the humanities whose weakening would be detrimental to preparing students and citizens for their civic responsibility. At the heart of liberal education lay the attainment of moral and intellectual virtue, the search for the common good, the capacity to free oneself from ignorance to increase the participation of citizens in the exercise of power and the democratization of society.

The contemplation of the universe (or *theoria, orao theion*, from "seeing the divine") also had for the Stoics a moral and political significance. It enabled observers to find their rightful place in the cosmic order, and learn how to live and act. The harmony and order of the universe served as a model for human conduct. Without being reduced to scientific understanding, *theoria* was associated with searching for a meaning of human existence and what was intrinsic about the world, a knowledge or logos that opened onto the realm of ethics and politics.

Since the sixth century BC, the liberal arts tradition related the contemplation of the cosmos with the harmonizing of one's soul. The Hellenistic education's curriculum encompassed on the one hand the Pythagorean *quadrivium* (arithmetic, geometry, astronomy, and music), and on the other, the *trivium* that included logic (the art of thinking), grammar (the art of inventing symbols), and rhetoric (the art of communicating).[10]

Seneca's opinions are no less relevant to and valuable for understanding current debates on the importance of the humanities today. Discussing in *Ad Lucilium Epistulae Morales* the significance of liberal education in the formation of virtuous characters, Seneca also highlighted the insufficiencies of vocational or professional training and the marketization of our universities:

"You have been wishing to know my views with regard to liberal studies. My answer is this: I respect no study and deem no study good, which results in money-making."[11]

He disdained any academic pursuit that could not lead to righteousness or virtue. Given that there existed different kinds of knowledge, he held the traditional Stoic view that philosophy was the discipline that was capable of conveying the good that encompassed both truth and virtue. The question of how the latter was acquired was central since Aristotle claimed that none of the moral qualities were present in us by nature.

According to Seneca, the study of language, poetry, philosophy, and music contributed to preparing the soul for the reception of virtue, and it enhanced the mind's ability to move toward it. Philosophy summed up for him the function of all the liberal arts disciplines. Beyond logic, dialectic, and rhetoric, students explored through it the principles of worthy action or praxis, "for philosophy could not exist without virtue, or virtue without philosophy."[12]

Higher education thus brought to light the human search for the principles of the universe (truth, science) and the practical moral response to such understanding (virtue, ethics). Its ultimate purpose was not as much knowledge or discourse as action and virtue. Seneca identified with Socrates for whom verity and virtue were the same, and he considered the study of philosophy and *studia liberalia* through the attainment of the highest good.

Since what took effect by chance was not an art and wisdom was an art, the latter should have a definite aim. The greatest aspiration and ultimate purpose of human existence was to uncover and give meaning to the relation that bonded the cosmos with its dwellers:

> Do you forbid me to contemplate the universe? Do you compel me to withdraw from the whole and restrict me to a part? May I not ask, what are the beginnings of all things, who molded the universe, who took the confused and conglomerate mass of sluggish matter and separated it into its parts? May I not inquire who is the Master-Builder of this universe, how the mighty bulk was brought under the control of law and order, who gathered together the scattered atoms, who separated the disordered elements and assigned an outward form to the elements that lay in one vast shapelessness?[13]

Beyond science, limited to an objective and materialistic knowledge of reality, Seneca conceived of the universe as a temple, a language to decipher in order to accede intelligibly and morally to the spectacle of Nature. This philosophical, poetic, and theological experience embodied the ultimate fulfillment of the humanities. Seneca believed that their emancipatory power could play a key role in the betterment of humanity.

From Plato to Seneca, philosophers explored the role of liberal education in the City and the place of individuals in society through the lenses of the cosmic order. Confronted with the skepticism and relativism of the Sophists, they privileged a form of instruction that formed the character and ethical disposition of students over professional or economic considerations. In doing so, they underscored the theoretical, existential, and sociopolitical ramifications of *studia liberalia*.

STUDIA HUMANITATIS AND REALPOLITIK

Beyond an education that pursues learning outcomes driven by economic, technical, or nonmoral ends, the humanities confront different sets of values that lead students to explore moral choices and what should be the aspirations of free individuals in society. Pico della Mirandola, Erasmus, and Machiavelli provided important insights in that regard on the question of human emancipation and what a free person should know in order to partake in the political life of society. Their views on education also reveal the extent to which some of today's most important issues confronting the humanities or *artes liberales* have not changed.

Questions relative to *studia humanitatis*' emancipationist virtues were continually explored in the Renaissance. Pico della Mirandola celebrated a divinely created humanity, which, liberated from the bonds of determinism, could become the modeler and sculptor of its own existence: "We have made you neither of heaven nor of earth, neither mortal nor immortal, so that you may, as the free and extraordinary shaper of yourself, fashion yourself in whatever form you prefer."[14] Contrary to other creatures, humans could choose and determine their fate according to their own free will.

Mirandola's manifesto situated humankind, measurer of all things, at the heart of Creation to ponder the meaning of its beauty and marvel at its vastness. This new position (at the time), which would seem very passé in many (albeit not all) academic circles today, entailed that humanity was responsible for its own existence and actions. Once it was brought into the world, it faced a primary moral choice: either degenerate or realize its true calling.

As moral and civic virtue were the aim of education, the humanistic tradition recognized the limits of an endless quest of learning for its own sake. Rabelais recounts how Gargantua called on his son Pantagruel to master the fields of world languages, history, law, and theology because they provided a broader understanding of the self and the world:

> I intend and will that you acquire a perfect command of languages [among them Greek, Latin, Hebrew, Chaldean and Arabic] [. . .]. Let there be no history which you do not hold ready in memory [. . .]. And for a few hours every day, start to study the Sacred Writings [. . .]. In short, let me see you an abyss of erudition.[15]

He also warned his son, however, that "science [or education] without conscience was but the ruination of the soul."[16] The word *conscience* entailed a moral choice and responsibility, which arguably today's students and faculty—regardless of their field—should make their own from quantitative to qualitative learning. As citizens, they can contribute either to the betterment or deterioration of society and to finding or not the "true calling" of humankind. The comprehension and contemplation of this moral choice rests on the study of the humanities.

The ultimate purpose of liberal education was and still is in some respects to provide training that inclines each individual to elevate his or her humanity. The latter word has become problematic today at least from a posthuman perspective. One was not born, according to Pico, but *became* human through learning from *studia humanitatis*. What Pico and Rabelais teach us through the idea of "consciousness" is that education involves moral choices.

In *Education of a Christian Prince*, Erasmus of Rotterdam pursued from this perspective his predecessors' reflections on governance and political leadership. According to Erasmus, the hope of a state lay in the proper education of its youth, and future political rulers needed to be guided toward the search for the common good: "The power should be entrusted to [the one] who excels all in the requisite qualities of wisdom, justice, moderation, foresight, and zeal for the public welfare."[17]

Erasmus subscribed to the ancient tradition of political thought originating from Plato and Aristotle. He also advocated a return to the principles of piety based on which the Christian ruler was to show three essential virtues: integrity, without which power led to tyranny; wisdom, whose alternative was destruction; and goodness, which needed to inspire the daily actions of political leaders.

The Christian prince had to abstain from inflicting harm upon the governed or being corrupted by bribes. The government office should not be a means of self-enrichment but bring about a relentless devotion to righteousness and the protection of its constituency. Toward these ends, a prince should be taught to rule beneficently.

Bridging humanistic education and the Christian faith, Erasmus contended that individuals endowed with free will were capable of forging the moral dimensions of their lives. He condemned in *The Praise of Folly* the hypocrisies and corruption of tyrannical kings and decadent clergymen who thrived on the ignorance of common people, affirming in light of Plato in *The Republic* that if a prince did not possess the qualities of a philosopher, he would be a tyrant.

Many corrupt leaders and their entourage in the sphere of power would benefit greatly from Erasmus's guidance today, not to mention the millions if not billions who suffer from the malevolence of their ruler. It should also be pointed out that Erasmus, who calls on the prince's "zeal for public welfare" in the exercise of power, makes no mention of the importance of becoming a master in economics or technology to become a "good prince."

A contrario, an acquisition of conscience and moral virtue through liberal education, was unwarranted for Machiavelli. The author of *The Prince* challenged the role of ethics in politics. Education did not necessarily provide a direct path to living a virtuous life, and the fact that happiness and fulfillment could be attained by behaving immorally cast a doubt on the relation between moral teaching and the individual or common good. Knowledge did not inevitably equate goodness, or lead to moral behavior.

Furthermore, the prince's power was not based on benevolence but anticipation and calculation. The mastery of the art of war and the defense of his State justified in this respect the use of all the means at his disposal. Removing from violence its immoral connotation, Machiavelli argued that a reputation for power that was not based upon one's own forces was unhealthy and undesirable.

In light of national and international political leadership today, Machiavelli is very much the philosopher of our time. Contrary to Erasmus's teaching, the Machiavellian prince advised not to be virtuous but to only give the appearance of being righteous by concealing one's real intentions. The exercise of virtue was in fact prejudicial to his dominion: "A man who wishes to profess goodness at all times will come to ruin among so many who are not good. Therefore, it is necessary for a prince who wishes to maintain himself in power to learn how not to be good, and to use this knowledge or not to use it according to necessity."[18]

The purpose of political leadership was not to ensure the common good through moral means, but to preserve one's power by all necessary measures. Machiavelli raised in this respect significant problems still relevant today, concerning the limits of education in a society when political leaders only aim at the conservation of power irrespective of ethical consideration and moral action.

Machiavelli's conception of political power brought about the end of this utopic vision of an ideal State ruled with virtue and justice: "Many writers have imagined republics and principalities that have never been seen nor known to exist in reality. For there is such a distance between how one lives and how one ought to live that anyone who abandons what is done for what ought to be done achieves his downfall rather than his preservation."[19]

Through this depiction of political power, it was not so much Machiavelli who was devoid of morality as the nature of human ambition that he portrayed, a reality made self-evident through history. The Italian thinker saw humans as creatures of passion, driven by an appetite for glory, wealth, and self-advancement. The pedagogical ideals of past philosophers were, according to him, based on the illusion that a virtuous education necessarily led to the betterment of human nature and society.

Machiavelli exemplified a skepticism similar to the Sophists in antiquity and, to some extent, to some postmodern thinkers today. In spite of the difference in their approaches, Pico, Rabelais, Erasmus, and Machiavelli demonstrated that education was ethical and political because it entailed moral choices. They each, like their Hellenic predecessors, contradicted Stanley Fish's assertion that the humanities were their own good and were of no pragmatic value in society.

CULTIVATING ALTERITY

Beyond a rationalistic, corporatist, and scientistic economic or STEM education, the justification and relevance of the humanities rests on the paths through which students explore and come to understand their humanity. Montaigne problematized in this respect the opposition between Erasmus and Machiavelli. He pondered the limits of self-knowledge, the relativity of vice and virtue, and the inconsistencies between doctrine and praxis. He furthermore confessed his inability to define what was ontologically proper to humankind:

> Others form man; I tell of him, and portray a particular one, very ill-formed, whom I should really make very different from what he is if I had to fashion him over gain. [. . .] Now the lines of my painting do not go astray though they change and vary. The world is but a perennial movement. All things in it are in constant motion [. . .]. I do not portray being: I portray passing. Not the passing from one age to another, or, as the people say, from seven years to seven years, but from day to day, from minute to minute. [. . .] If my mind could gain a firm footing, I would not make essays, I would make decisions; but it is always in apprenticeship and on trial.[20]

In a state of perpetual motion and changing sensorial experience, trying to understand human nature through reason was like attempting to seize water with bare hands. It was vain in this context to believe that the acquisition of knowledge would make humans necessarily virtuous:

> In truth, knowledge is a great and very useful quality; those who despise it give evidence enough of their stupidity. But yet I do not set its value at that extreme measure that some attribute to it, like Herillus the philosopher, who placed in it the sovereign good, and held that it was in its power to make us wise and content. That I do not believe, nor what others have said, that knowledge is the mother of all virtue, and that all vice is produced by ignorance. If that is true, it is subject to a long interpretation.[21]

Also, one could find among Renaissance writers until Montaigne a distinction between *homo*, pertaining to the biological species, and *humanitas*, the essence or state of worthiness that humankind was called to reach. It was through culture, the arts, and literary education that the *homo* became *humanus* and developed its unique ability to become human in the noblest sense of the word. According to Classical beliefs, a human being not trained in rhetoric, poetry, or Greco-Latin literature could not ascend to its full humanity, which was its dignity.

Montaigne introduced a new problematic that still reverberates in our modern and postmodern age. In addition to undoing the relation of knowledge/virtue and opposition of *homo/humanitas*, he stressed that schooling ought not to be so focused on what we know as *how* we know and learn.

Before Montaigne, Rabelais highlighted the need for a universal comprehensive education. According to this vision, an individual needed physical, intellectual, and spiritual training to be fully "humanized" or civilized. Another path illustrated by Pico della Mirandola asserted that humankind conquered its grandeur through its conversion to God.

As the distinction between *homo* and *humanus* lost its relevance from a Western perspective, human fulfillment was no longer sought or achieved through becoming "complete" or "educated." For Montaigne, being human alone was what elevated the individual to a state of worthiness, each living individual bearing the entire form of the human condition.

To appreciate the political significance of his views on education and for individuals and society, one should consider that humanity (and thus *humanitas*) lost with Montaigne the assurance of its domination over nature as illustrated in Plutarch and Lucretius's *De Rerum Natura*. Through his "dialogues" with ancient philosophers, he sought examples in other human cultures and experiences that would help him situate and stimulate his reflection and judgment.

In an early critique of ethnocentrism, he recognized the arbitrary nature of human customs and beliefs and thus felt compelled to confront his views with others' reality: "He who contradicts me, teaches me," he wrote in "Of the Art of Discussion."[22]

Beyond the impasse and limits of self-knowledge and representation, Montaigne recognized the essential pedagogical value of approaching textual and societal issues through alterity and intertextuality. The writing of *Essays* had significant political and theoretical implications in this respect for it foresaw the emergence of current critical approaches to literature and human experience such as postcolonial and cross-cultural studies.

For example, in "On Coaches" and "Of Cannibals," Montaigne squarely put in question the assumed superiority of Western culture over others, and he highlighted the need to acknowledge and investigate the diversity of human experience. By doing so, he opposed educators who promoted a form of self-centered pedantry and conveyed their knowledge in a vain and presumptuous manner:

> In truth, most of the time, they seem to have sunk even beneath common sense. [. . .] They know the theory of all things; *you* find someone who will put it in practice. [. . .] They understand neither themselves nor others. [. . .] They have a full enough memory but an entirely hollow judgment [. . .].[23]

This criticism revealed the importance Montaigne granted to the need for a renewed and transformed learning experience to have a concrete impact on self and society: "Now, it is not enough for our education not to spoil us; it must change us for the better."[24]

Regretting that students did not learn for life but for the schoolroom or the marketplace, such as in today's technical and professional training, the essayist lamented that this type of erudition had no bearing on the conduct of young people and future citizens. It was essential to ask who was better learned rather than ask who was more learned.

Learning could not be an end in itself. One ought not educate through hearsay alone but through deed; by training not only through words and precepts but also toward moral achievement: "Now that the learned have appeared, good men are wanting. Any other knowledge is harmful to a man who has not the knowledge of goodness."[25]

Through the practice of critical thinking, and the transfer from ethical thought into moral action, a student was best prepared to exercise his or her freedom, be emancipated from ignorance and prejudice, and exercise judgment toward the formation of a more open and altruistic society:

> I would rather make of him an able man than a learned man. I would also urge that care be taken to choose a guide with a well-made rather than well-filled head. [. . .] The gain from our study is to have become better and wiser by it. [. . .] Among the liberal arts, let us begin with the art that liberates us. [. . .] What sense have I if I can amuse myself with the secret of the stars, having death or slavery ever present before my eyes? [. . .] He who does otherwise seems to say that it is not yet time to live happily, or that it is no longer time.[26]

The author and former mayor of Bordeaux clearly associated the purpose of education, and specifically liberal education, with the achievement of the good and the betterment of humanity. Through this relation, he underscored the importance of acquiring empathy, and highlighted the political significance and value of critical thinking, cross-cultural awareness, and interdisciplinary approaches to learning.

Finally, Montaigne contended that students and teachers alike should concede to the limits of their knowledge and consequently search for and develop increased attentiveness to alterity. This change that shed a new light on what constitutes human subjectivity, as well as progress and virtuous governance, called for a renewed inquiry about the nature of education in theory and practice.

From a political perspective, it anticipated the emergence of the Enlightenment and modern democracy. Sympathetic to liberal values, Montaigne notably asserted in "On Repentance" that people of all origins shared a common nature and that each individual bore the entire form of the human condition.

At a time when the boundaries between the rational and irrational, knowledge and belief, became unclear, Montaigne adamantly contended that education, and specifically the humanities, should change humans for the better. His pedagogy called for a renewed moral compass that could guide perfectible individuals toward an increased attentiveness to difference.

THE POSTMODERN AND UTILITARIAN CHALLENGE

The emergence of postmodern skepticism about truth, progress, and the possibility of objective knowledge, the rejection of totalities and universal values, and the end of ideals and grand historical narratives has made it challenging to claim that the humanities do matter for society's advancement.

A precursor of the postmodern, Friedrich Nietzsche embodied the rupture with modern humanism's belief in progress and challenged the tenets of liberal education: "The last thing *I* would promise would be to 'improve' mankind. No new idols will be erected by me; the old may learn what feet of clay they have."[27] He condemned the illusion of creating what he considered to be an idealized fictional world that would be better than the one here and now.

The postmodern impediment that he foresaw announced queries on the subject of higher education that still resonate today. To the question *Is it desirable or even possible to "improve" humankind or society?* Nietzsche answered by the negative. But even if we contemplate that a positive answer is possible, we are faced with another challenge: Whose morals should one follow in higher education to inculcate and shape the proper character of students?

These questions open up to the realm of polity, or societal governance, in the sense that they address who decides or who should decide what counts as knowledge and what is "just," and/or morality. They posit a norm that may exclude anyone who does not meet it in the participation of the making of a given society.

They also entail a pedagogical reflection. Should higher education be limited to the sphere of intellectual rather than moral virtue? Should more emphasis be given to the vocational benefits of education and liberal education abandoned? This change would inevitably enhance the rise of scientific, technical, and professional academic disciplines, and only corroborate, like Stanley Fish, that the humanities have no contributory values, only intrinsic worth, and that they should not be regarded as instrumental to some larger good.

Beyond the notion that knowledge may be inculcated for its own sake, liberal education's societal and global significance need to be recognized and revealed. More than schooling based on purely economic or technological usefulness, it is conducive to raising moral and intellectual inquiries that sharpen the critical capacities of students. The former prepares the individual for a specific task or practice that has utilitarian value while the latter demands a reflection about the students' place and responsibility in society and the world—socially, civically, and existentially.

More than the fields of science, technology, or economics, and contrary to Stanley Fish's pessimism on the subject, the humanities can enable and foster the debate on what constitutes the "larger good" and how to aim toward it. In this respect, higher education cannot solely revolve, as it does increasingly today, around technical or utilitarian values and market measurements and the emancipatory nature of the humanities—their capacity to address and explore social, cultural, societal, and political concerns, both intellectually and ethically—must be central to any educational experience.

The current state of the political world today is dramatic. Globally, the number of people affected by humanitarian crises has almost doubled in the past decade. Those displaced by conflict exceeds fifty-one million, the highest number since World War II. Economic crises leading to poverty and inequality, climate change, nuclear threats resulting from scientific and technological development, gun and gender violence, forced migration, human trafficking—these are daily reminders that we live in societies marked by financial, environmental, and existential predicaments.

The world is still very much a "work in progress" for the most optimistic, if we take as an example the Universal Declaration of Human Rights, adopted at the UN Assembly in 1948. Only twenty full democracies exist out of 167 countries according to the democracy index by regime type. Corruption is rampant in the vast majority of the remaining countries in which the role of parliament, the independence of the judiciary, and free access to public information and the media is continuously undermined.

Meanwhile, the growing marketization and technicization of universities is weakening models of education based on emancipationist humanism at a time when in a generation, interest in civic responsibility has dramatically worsened. As a UCLA-administered survey indicates, all values consistent with being a good citizen and active participant in the democratic life of the City are on the decline while the number of students who major in vocational and professional disciplines have risen at an accelerating pace in recent years.

More than ever, higher education needs to offer alternative ways of thinking, challenge ways of knowing, interrogate sources of information, create a context for counternarrative, and foster the conditions for change. In the words of bell hooks:

> We need educators to make schools places where the conditions for democrat-
> ic consciousness can be established and flourish. [. . .] The future of demo-
> cratic education will be determined by the extent to which democratic values
> can triumph over the spirit of oligarchy that seek to silence diverse voices. [28]

Overcoming the postmodern and utilitarian challenge implies the realization that education through teaching and learning is political and shapes
society. This is particularly true if we consider, from a humanities' perspective, that it entails a reflection and decision about what counts as knowledge,
which curriculum content is worthy of attention and research, and how to
approach it pedagogically. Paolo Freire, Henry Giroux, and bell hooks,
among others, have argued that knowledge is socially produced and determined by strategies of exclusion or containment. They discussed in particular
the importance of acquiring critical consciousness through education, and the
sociopolitical relevance of literature and criticism.

The role of the humanities is precisely to struggle against and overcome
the forms of education and power that can transform someone into an object
and instrument through the sphere of knowledge, truth, and discourse. In the
words of Fredric Jameson, the only effective liberation from an illusory
psychological project of salvation "begins with the recognition that there is
nothing that is not social and historical—indeed, that everything is in the last
analysis political." [29]

BEYOND BORDERS: BETTERING HUMANITY

Montaigne's vision of the possible betterment of individuals and society
through liberal education is still relevant to our postmodern age. It demands
the preparation of future generations to best exercise their freedom through
critical thinking, and thus be emancipated from ignorance, prejudice, and
given knowledge. Beyond the limits of self-knowledge, Montaigne called on
us to reconsider the proper schooling for the member of the polis with a
critical outlook attentive to difference.

Raising questions pertaining to the aim of liberal education, he examined
a series of contentious issues that foretold modern and postmodern inquiries
on the subject: to what extent could or should it foster moral virtue and
"improve humankind," to use Nietzsche's cynical expression? Should it be
an end in itself or serve ideal or political purposes for the betterment of
humanity?

Before Montaigne attested to the crisis of subjective representation, Aristotle already conceded to the relativity of truth, values, and ethical norms and

its implications for education. The author of *Nicomachean Ethics* lived with the realization that the objective world depended on the perceiving individual and that the concepts of virtue, justice, and goodness were relative entities. This recognition did not, however, lead him to abandon his inquiry into the human good.

Privileging alterity, Montaigne also continued his search for a more just, better world. And in *Essay Concerning Human Understanding*, Locke's argument that the human mind's content and faculty were determined by the imprinted perceptions derived from experience did not give up either. Recognizing that arbitrary sensations were at the source of rational ideas and knowledge, Locke continued to inquire about what a possible future democratic ideal for humankind might be.

In spite of their different social status, he believed that individuals possessed unalienable rights that governments should not violate. In this imagined society, the philosopher guided the magistrate to assess what was just and unjust and the sovereign to assess the origins and limits of authority. Locke advocated toleration, a concern for equality, and individual liberty. He also recognized, like Montaigne, the moral and emancipatory role of critical learning: "Of all the men we meet with, nine parts of ten are what they are, good or evil, useful or not, by their education."[30]

Montaigne's new pedagogic approaches—no longer focusing on what we learn and know but *how* we do so—gave his work a political dimension. Questioning the foundations of knowledge did not lead Montaigne to abandon his search for a link between education and the betterment of individuals and society. It changed the orientation of his thinking toward the "other" and expanded possibilities for argumentation and dialogue.

By inquiring about received assumptions, Montaigne transgressed the boundaries between self and others, but also those between academic disciplines. In doing so, he imparted a political and social dimension to his teaching. Transformative and emancipatory, his approach partakes in the democratization of the educational experience and society. In the words of Henry Giroux:

> The question of how we learn to become subjects engages not only our own self formation but the possibilities for society at any given time. How does one come to self-understanding? How does one situate oneself in history? How do we relate questions of knowledge to power? How do we understand the limitations of our institutions, or even our age?[31]

Attentive to alterity and difference, Montaigne created the pedagogical condition to interrogate the epistemological margins that structure knowledge. From theoretical issues to practical concerns, he proposed a reflection in which the question of the other preempts that of truth. Education's purpose was still for him the betterment of self and society. Montaigne initiated a movement reaching to Dewey and Richard Rorty for whom the crisis of postmodernity did not set in motion the abandonment of the Enlightenment political aspirations.

Conversely, by privileging fragmentation, aporia, and playfulness, a form of postmodernism or anti-foundationalism that in absolute terms denies the possible link between education and society constitutes an important but rather limited means of academic inquiry. How could anyone, from the latter perspective, assess or make any claim about the importance of the humanities or its relevance for the functioning of democracy? How could one speak about what constitutes human rights or the betterment of individuals? How could one assess the path to the common good, or claim anything at all?

A critic of such postmodern expression, Fredric Jameson observed that it led to an "increased occultation of the class struggle" and an inability to link the "concerns of private life with the confines of affluent society."[32]

It should be pointed out here that Jean-François Lyotard's questioning of metanarratives that attempt to explain the totality of human experience did not probe so much the possibility of knowledge as its source and purpose (who decides what it is, how, and why). As such, the valorization of micro-narratives (from minorities, the poor, subaltern, and disenfranchised) that he promoted echoed the Foucauldian understanding that human knowledge, thought, and action are shaped by political and socioeconomic reality.

A liberal education based on *paideia* for the betterment of individuals and society can become problematic in that regard when it is rooted in concepts such as goodness, truth, and being, defined by a few and presumed to be universal. More than any other academic field, however, the humanities convey through the search for intellectual and moral virtue the capacity to reflect and think critically in order to address this predicament.

Far beyond the traditional and current pedagogical approaches to teaching economics, science, and technology, the humanities foster a reflection about the aims of education and its political ramifications for society; what constitutes an ethical or moral response to the existential challenges of our times; and how to continue to think and write critically in a postmodern context. According to Henry Giroux, "A critical pedagogy for democracy does not begin with test scores but with questions. What kinds of citizens do we hope to produce through public education in a postmodern culture?"[33]

Education is political and shapes society because decisions about what counts as knowledge are made in the classroom and dominant discourses affect consciousness and orient students to think, feel, speak, and act in specific ways. Through feminist, postcolonial, Marxist, or queer theory, to give a few examples, critical teaching and thinking lead both the educators and educated to be social critics, and question what constitutes economic and social justice, political rights and responsibilities, and thus democratic life.

In the United States, this intellectual, political, and moral endeavor in liberal education resulted from the Proclamation of the Constitution that guaranteed equal status before the law for individual citizens, and more recently the civil rights movement that culminated in the 1964 Civil Rights Act and the Voting Rights Act of 1965.

It is revealing that in an article published in 1947 in the Morehouse College student paper, *The Maroon Tiger*, titled "The Purpose of Education," the eighteen-year-old Martin Luther King Jr. argued that the function of education was to teach one "to think intensively and critically." Education that stopped with efficiency, he contended, would prove "the greatest menace to society."

Intelligence alone was not enough, he reflected; it needed character to embody what should be the goal of true education. It is edifying to consider that, a few years later, the leader of the civil rights movement and peace activist put the notion of character at the heart of his Washington, D.C., address at the Lincoln Memorial: "I Have a Dream."

Chandra Mohanty explored in *Feminist Genealogies, Colonial Legacies, Democratic Futures* the political dimensions of critical thinking when considering the interconnection between gender, class, and colonialism. Echoing the thought of W. E. B. Du Bois, she highlighted the emancipatory dimension of liberal education that she perceived as a key strategy of decolonization rather than upward mobility that a professional education would provide.

In the words of Adrienne Rich, thinking critically means refusing to accept what is given, "listening and watching in art and literature, in the social sciences, in all the descriptions we are given of the world, for the silences, the absences, the nameless, the unspoken, the encoded."[34]

From the works of antiquity to the more recent feminist, postcolonial, queer, Marxist, or psychoanalytical studies, students, teachers, authors, and critics affiliated with the humanities explore and respond to the pressing challenges facing human existence. Openness to all critical attitudes, including deconstruction, engages students to debate, think critically, and explore issues from broader perspectives.

More than any other fields of studies, the humanities provide a breadth of critical approaches that enable students to raise their level of awareness and comprehension of what it means to be human and partake in civic engagement. Aristotle and Derrida but also music, art, theater, or poetry teach us valuable lessons about the academic and political reality bridging the university, self, and society.

The issues and challenges of our times are many in the United States and beyond: the economic, financial, political, and environmental crises; the limits and danger of scientific and technological progress; the lack of virtuous political leadership and understanding among people of different cultures and religions; poverty; inequality; racism; human trafficking; and violence, to name just a few.

The humanities enable us to see beyond these challenges. Many authors, thinkers, and philosophers (or artists, poets, painters, and musicians) since antiquity fundamentally questioned and imagined how society and the world could and should be. Plato and Aristotle provided an essential point of departure in the search for the individual and collective good in theocratic and aristocratic societies, as did the Renaissance authors, poets, and artists who reconceived the paths toward virtue and the ends of human life in an infinite universe seemingly devoid of meaning.

What will be our legacy for those who will inhabit Earth in the next centuries? What paths will we have shown to future generations? The humanities constitute an essential treasure that must be enriched and transmitted not only because they inspire us and give meaning to our lives but also because they make us think about the necessity and the means to construct a better world for ourselves and others.

Bridging the university and society requires, as John Dewey contended in *Democracy and Education*, the formation of an educated citizenry that understands its social and political responsibilities. A world in crisis demands that the humanities be brought back to the heart of university life. What sociological, ethical, political, and/or critical role can be left to play for individuals in society?

Given that in our postmodern and posthuman world, economics, science, and technology have been elevated to a quasi-sacred form of religion, and that cyborgs, clones, and robots have allegedly altered the human condition, what response can the humanities provide? Asking this question leads precisely to where the humanities' and humanity's fate and future are at stake and become one.

NOTES

1. Martha Nussbaum, *Not for Profit: Why Democracy Needs the Humanities* (Princeton, NJ: Princeton University Press, 2010), 2.
2. Aristotle, *Nicomachean Ethics*, translated by Robert C. Bartlett and Susan D. Collins (Chicago: University of Chicago Press, 2011), xi.
3. Aristotle, *Nicomachean Ethics*, xii.
4. Plato, *The Republic*, translated by Desmond Lee (New York: Penguin Classic, 2007), xx.
5. Plato, *The Republic*, 529d .
6. Plato, *The Republic*, 473d–e.
7. Sheramy D. Bundrick, *Music and Image in Classical Athens* (Cambridge: Cambridge University Press, 2005), 60.
8. Aristotle, *Politics* , translated by Carnes Lord (Chicago: University of Chicago Press, 2013), 1332a, 210.
9. Plato, *The Republic*, 1095b, 7.

10. David Knowles, *The Evolution of Medieval Thought*, ed. D. E. Luscombe and C. N. L. Brooke (London: Longman Group Limited, 1988), 56.

11. Seneca, *Ad Lucilium Epistulae Morales*, translated by Richard M. Gummere (Cambridge: Harvard University Press, 1967), Ep. LXXXVIII, 349.

12. Seneca, *Ad Lucilium Epistulae Morales*, Ep. LXXXIX, 381–83.

13. Seneca, *Ad Lucilium Epistulae Morales*, Ep. LXV, 455.

14. Pico della Mirandola, *Oration on the Dignity of Man*, eds. Francesco Borghesi, Michael Papio, and Massimo Riva (New York: Cambridge University Press, 2012), 117.

15. François Rabelais, *Gargantua and Pantagruel*, translated by M. A. Screech (New York: Penguin Classics, 2006), 48–49.

16. Rabelais, *Gargantua and Pantagruel*, 49.

17. Erasmus of Rotterdam, *Education of a Christian Prince*, translated by Lester K. Born (New York: Columbia University Press, 1968), 140.

18. Niccolo Machiavelli, *The Prince*, translated by Peter Bondanella (New York: Oxford University Press, 2008), 53.

19. Machiavelli, *The Prince*, 53.

20. Michel de Montaigne, "Of Repentance," *Essays*, III, 2, *The Complete Essays of Montaigne* translated by Donald M. Frame (Stanford, CA: Stanford University Press, 1976), 610–11.

21. Montaigne, "Apology for Raymond Sebond," II, 12, 319.

22. Montaigne, "Of the Art of Discussion," III, 8, 205.

23. Montaigne, "Of Pedantry," I, 25, 102.

24. Montaigne, "Of Pedantry," 103.

25. Montaigne, "Of Pedantry," 103, 105.

26. Montaigne, "Of the Education of Children," I, 26, 110–21.

27. Friedrich Nietzsche, *Ecce Homo: How One Becomes What One Is*, translated by Thomas Wayne (New York: Algora Publishing, 2004), 8.

28. bell hooks, *Teaching Critical Thinking, Practical Wisdom* (New York: Routledge, 2010), 17.

29. Fredric Jameson, *The Political Unconscious* (Ithaca, NY: Cornell University Press, 1981), 20.

30. John Locke, *Some Thoughts Concerning Education*, Part 1 (Mineola, NY: Dover Philosophical Classic, 2007), 21.

31. Henry Giroux, *Border Crossings: Cultural Workers and the Politics of Education* (London: Routledge, 2005), 12.

32. Fredric Jameson, *Postmodernism, or, the Cultural Logic of Late Capitalism* (Durham, NC: Duke University Press, 1991), xvi.

33. Giroux, *Border Crossings*, 74.

34. Adrienne Rich, *On Lies, Secrets, and Silence* (New York: W. W. Norton Company, 1979), 244–45.

Chapter Two

Humanizing Economics

In his 2013 presidential address at the MLA, Michael Bérubé stated: "There are only two things you can say in Washington when it comes to foreign language study. One is that it will enhance our economic competitiveness abroad; the other is that it will be critical to national security."[1] This observation raised a fundamental question: "Why should anyone bother with advanced studies in the humanities?"[2]

Its historical sources and purpose partly lay in Socrates's idea that an examined life should liberate the mind from the bondage of custom and habit. The philosopher promoted living a life in which all beliefs should be questioned and the ability to reason should be nurtured. From this perspective, the liberal arts inherited centuries of philosophical tradition that explored the life of the mind, the human condition, and the knowledge of languages and cultures.

The word *liberalis* had two connotations in ancient Rome. One referred to freeborn individuals who were dissuaded from exercising critical thinking; the other, favored by Seneca, concerned the instruction of all citizens, regardless of their class status, so that they could lay claim to their own minds.

THE MARKET AND LIBERAL EDUCATION

The greatest challenge to the latter vision in recent years has been economic in nature. In a competitive, technical, and commercial environment, the humanities have been forced at times to abandon one of its most valuable ambitions. With the recent economic downturn, the usefulness of a degree in liberal arts has been increasingly questioned: it allegedly does not bear measurable or quantifiable advantages for the students entering the job market.

Academics such as Derek Bok and Andrew Delbanco have criticized in this respect the recent trend toward the marketization of the university. Much to their regret, humanities programs have been readily threatened with amputation, if not extinction, and are "expected to prostrate themselves before economic rationales in their struggles for survival."[3] Emblematic of this development, Jim Leach, former chairman of the National Endowment for the Humanities, described the humanities as essential to revitalize the American productivity engine.

We would contend that the purpose of the liberal arts should not revolve around the regression or resurgence of economic activity, and that they do not exist at the expense of economic well-being. Furthermore, taking into account the breadth of critical thinking and ethical considerations they provide, they should play a greater role in the teaching of the social sciences, specifically economics.

To support this claim, it should be pointed out that, according to a study by Michael Dewilde, heads of companies often privilege students and job candidates who have a background in liberal arts education over business: "[They] want to work with a staff that is smart and articulate, with people who have breadth, depth, and character, and who are intellectually curious, not terrified by change, and willing, with a little nudge, to engage at least a little in what Socrates referred to as 'the examined life.'"[4]

Without denying the importance of preparing students for professional life and the contribution made by the humanities in this respect, one should question whether the sole purpose of education, and specifically liberal education, should be to prepare students for the marketplace. Narrowing the scope of its aim to utilitarian values imperils Seneca's vision that all citizens be trained in the arts, literature, philosophy, and critical thinking so that they can call their minds their own.

Equally important, liberal education offers students a much broader view and understanding of human experience than other academic disciplines like economics that often solely rely on quantifiable data and mathematical models. The premise of my argument here is that economics' pedagogical content should be questioned and challenged not only for the problems it poses to society but also the future of humanity.

The critical assets the humanities can offer students in this respect are invaluable. They should be measured beyond the gauge of marketability in noneconomic—that is, societal and existential—terms. They include cultivating the ability to think critically and training for good citizenship.

Making the case for the humanities thus calls for a reflection on not only what but also how we teach, how we can foster moral virtue and convey to the future participants of society a sense of civic responsibility, more than any economic or scientific discipline alone ever could.

Is a wealthy society that leaves so many of its members in poverty humanly acceptable? For many economists, inequality is the price to pay for economic growth. They adhere to the rules of a competitive international system in which thousands are dying of hunger every day. It is revealing that in the social sciences, economics is the field of study that uses mathematics the most in its attempt to measure the production and distribution of resources available in society and to determine the proper courses of economic policies.

At least two different approaches are possible when one wants to study social phenomena: either take as a point of departure the individual's choices by themselves, or consider the historical and environmental contexts in which these choices are made. The first approach is adopted by mainstream economic theory known as "neoclassical," as part of what is commonly called "microeconomics." The second, which is emphasized in the works of Smith, Marx, and Keynes, among others, relates to the field of "macroeconomics."

The proponents of the neoclassical approach to economics introduce "the market" as an abstract entity that should be explored mathematically according to the laws of supply and demand. Its detractors underscore the hypothetical and speculative nature of the works of mathematicians, who, as "experts," pile up equations based on assumptions that are distant from the concrete societal economic problems.

In contrast with a pedagogy that fosters the use of mathematics in the teaching of economics, we need to explore how the study of literature and history reveal the extent to which prevailing discourses of economics are institutionally constructed, how they are inseparable from the cultural and political realm, and how they are the product of social forces.

Critiquing and illuminating the nature of economics thus demands a broad reflection that must be open to interdisciplinary perspectives, including the humanities. As an example, the economist John Maynard Keynes discussed how psychology and economics were intrinsically related via the unfulfilled human desire for money and the relentless accumulation of capital.

Keynes believed that, like every citizen, an economist should fully participate in the political and social life of society, and needed for that purpose a humanistic education. He criticized economists' predispositions to justify laissez-faire policies and condemned the existence of recurrent economic discourses based on ahistorical considerations such as the law of the market, competition, and efficiency, which led inevitably to the exacerbation of social injustice.

He also questioned the foundations of economics based on the laws of nature and rejected the use of mathematics that in his view was either contingent or historically determined, and above all a language that ensured the logic of its own reasoning.

In contrast with orthodox (or "neoclassical") economists who asserted the scientific nature of their methodical approach and the exactness of the laws it revealed, Keynes considered that "too large a proportion of recent 'mathematical' economics are merely concoctions, as imprecise as the initial assumptions they rest on, which allow the author to lose sight of the complexities and interdependencies of the real world in a maze of pretentious and unhelpful symbols."[5]

John Maynard Keynes's argument helps us identify the value of humanizing economics through the liberal arts. It suggests that society and human relations cannot be fully analyzed and understood through mathematics alone as these relationships are embedded in historical contexts and moral considerations.

The recent financial crisis demonstrated that mathematic models were not representative of the real world and that the dehumanization of economic discourse called for the reintroduction of moral, political, and philosophical inquiries to meet the social and environmental challenges of our time.

As the financial world threatens to collapse, economic decisions must take into account ethical considerations, and put human needs at the heart of its concerns. Considering the current rise of poverty and unemployment in the industrialized world in addition to the problem of accumulated debt reaching $20 trillion in the United States alone, economics is proving to be a science in crisis. Yet the unchallenged logic of the market continues to dominate its pedagogical discourse to a degree unprecedented since the Industrial Revolution.

The following will illustrate the gap that exists between the teaching of economics in universities and the real economic experience of people around the world today. While so much wealth has never before been produced, basic needs of hundreds of millions are being ignored around the world.

According to Oxfam International, about 1.3 billion people have at their disposal less than a dollar a day to survive. During the last decade of the twentieth century, global income increased by an average of 2.5 percent per year while the actual number of poor people has increased by more than one hundred million. In 1998, the number of people living on less than $2 a day were in the order of 2.8 billion.

As stated by a 2001 report prepared by the United Nations Development Program, 1 percent of the world's richest people received a combined income equal to that of the poorest 57 percent. The alter-globalization militants pointed out that between 1990 and 2000, despite a substantial increase of GDP worldwide, the number of people suffering from hunger and malnutrition had not changed significantly, averaging a total of ten million deaths per year, nearly twenty-five thousand per day, according to the World Food Program.[6]

Concerning inequality, the combined wealth of the richest 1 percent will overtake that of everyone else by next year given the current trends. The richest 1 percent have seen their share of global wealth increase from 44 percent in 2009 to 48 percent in 2014 and will likely surpass 50 percent in 2016.

Of the remaining global wealth, "almost all is owned by the rest of the richest fifth of the world's population. The other 80 percent share just 5.5 percent and have an average wealth of $3,851 per adult—that's 1/700th of the average wealth of the 1%. Meanwhile, 1 in 9 people do not have enough to eat and more than a billion people still live on less than $1.25 a day."[7]

Faced with these challenges, it is essential to conceive alternate economic rationales that take into account real-life experiences and the consequences of economic policy. This reconceptualization that begins in the classroom can only be achieved by humanizing the acquisition of economic principles through an acute understanding of history, its effects on people, and the reading of literature (e.g., novels) in order to develop students' critical abilities as well as their senses of empathy.

UNCOVERING THE RHETORIC OF ECONOMICS

Countering the phenomenon of exclusion and inequality and improving the living conditions of the majority around the world also necessitates a reflection on the language of economics itself. In a study published in 1983, Deirdre McCloskey argued first that the study of economics fell within the realm of literary criticism; second, that mathematical models, valued by economists, were essentially metaphorical and poetic; and third, that economists were late by an epistemological revolution (e.g., the emergence of poststructuralism and anti-foundationalism) when they claimed to rely on their scientific assurance and authority.

McCloskey's *The Rhetoric of Economics* has become a classic in the field of economic methodology. Demystifying the official scientific discourse of mainstream economics, the book sparked a heated argument and opened a new field of research. McCloskey sought to demonstrate that economists, like all scientists, often unconsciously developed a rhetoric of façade to confer a scientific validity to their findings.

McCloskey defined the term *rhetoric* as "the art of proving what one believes to be true, not what is true from an abstract method" or, more simply, the art of persuasion, and she saw economists as poets who use and rely on figures of speech, especially metaphors, to convince others. Like all scientists, she contended, economists also have a talent for storytelling. All science relies on logic and facts but also metaphors and narratives. If the first two were part of the official discourse of science, the last two, equally important and indispensable, fell within the realm of the humanities.

McCloskey underscored in this regard the fictional, relative, and literary dimensions of economics, even when it had recourse to mathematics. Countering the economist viewpoint that the "law of demand" was compelling, she argued that the latter's foundations fit within the "scientific" paradigm because of statistics and testing, yet also fell outside the scope of science because of its reliance upon introspection and analogy.

Using Saussure, she drew a parallel between economic analysis and the synchronic (considering language as timeless) and diachronic (taking into account its development through history). In economics, she asserted, one could also find such a duality at play: to the ahistorical, static, and abstract dimension of economics corresponded a historical and dynamic one.

Studying the history of the "language" of economics enabled her to explore how the "mathematization" of its discourse emerged through the import of positivist thinking marked by the guiding principles of testability, quantification, and objectivity. The problem underscored here is that when economists began to blindly adopt these modernist precepts they had already been challenged by Thomas S. Kuhn, who in *The Structures of Scientific Revolution* questioned the notion of progress in scientific knowledge.

In light of Paul K. Feyerabend who recently undermined the presumed universal, objective, and methodological foundations of scientific theory, McCloskey proposed abandoning the idea of methodology conceived from a positivist perspective, encouraging instead the instauration of a "dialogue" between paradigms and among scientists. It is through a rigorous rhetorical analysis, she claimed, that one could best understand the development of science and economics, more specifically, through the actual conversations between scientists.

Her groundbreaking work falls here within the realm of the humanities and constitutes from this standpoint a reference for anyone in the social sciences or liberal arts who aims at deconstructing any positivist interpretation of economics to enable a better understanding of the history of the discipline. The demystification of economic science constitutes an important first step toward humanizing economics.

Economics belongs to the field of history but also of language, rhetoric, and discourse. Under the scope of the historical field, one could analyze how the successive phases of economic thought related to the intellectual and social mores of their time. One can grasp within the sphere of the humanities how it was linguistically and rhetorically constructed through the ideas, feelings, and thoughts generated by the political and social climate of a given era.

This is what Joseph A. Schumpeter's *History of Economic Analysis* reveals by situating the development of economic thought from ancient Greece to the present in its intellectual and ideological context, taking into account the philosophical, psychological, and sociological dimensions of the subject.

We learn, for example, that for Xenophon (426–354 BC) the term *economics* was associated with the art of administering households (which in Green theory extends to planet Earth), and that for Aristotle and Plato economic practices should be restrained to the bare minimum for fear that they further chrematistics, the uncontrolled accumulation of money for its own sake, which dehumanized and threatened the stability of the City. Economics should in their view be submitted to a polity, itself subjected to morals.

During the Renaissance and the modern period, economics gradually came to be independent of morality and politics' influence as it ascended to scientific autonomy. Its entity rested on natural laws comparable to the ones discovered in Newtonian physics and mechanics, and the foundations of "pure economics" fell into the black hole of mathematics.

Until the sixteenth century, economics was conceived as an extension of philosophical, historical, or political analysis. Its significance gradually began to emerge as an independent discipline until the nineteenth century when alternative theories (reformism, socialism, Marxism) to the traditional paradigms were used to argue for a statewide action to regulate its activities. One can attest today to the coexistence of several competing paradigms such as neoclassicism, Keynesianism, and libertarianism.

Asked why we should study the history of economics, Schumpeter underscored the pedagogical advantages of studying how new ideas and insights were brought into the human mind. Without such inquiry, students would experience a lack of direction and meaning.

In effect, Schumpeter argues that current issues cannot be grasped without knowledge of previous issues since scientific analysis is neither a logically consistent process nor does it lead to a progressive discovery of an objective reality. It represents rather an "incessant struggle with creations of our own and our predecessors' minds": "The state of any science at any given time implies its past history and cannot be satisfactorily conveyed without making this implicit history explicit."[8]

John Maynard Keynes also highlighted the importance of possessing a good knowledge of the history of thought: "The ideas of economists and political philosophers, both when they are right and when they are wrong, are more powerful than is commonly understood. Indeed the world is ruled by little else. Practical men, who believe themselves to be quite exempt from any intellectual influence, are usually the slaves of some defunct economist. Madmen in authority, who hear voices in the air, are distilling their frenzy from some academic scribbler of a few years back."[9]

Keynes also alludes here to the critical importance of liberal education, and to the ideal that all citizens should lay claim to their own minds and be liberated from the bondage of unquestioned assumptions.

More recently, Philip Mirowski examined how the process of legitimization of economic discourse was determined through the collective heritage of a given society, including its structure of law, order, and system of power. An understanding of this development thus required a deeper reflection on the complex history of the relationship between economics and politics.

Our contemporary society is confronted daily with a broad range of information, ideas, opinions, and questions pertaining to economic strategy; the importance given to economic issues reflects the urgency of the many problems we face today. The debates and diverse contentions concern the choice of policies on public debt management, the financing of health and educational systems, minimum wages, labor relations, and unlimited growth and the danger it represents for the preservation of the environment.

While these issues involve economic decisions, they cannot be left in the hands of economists alone given the importance they bear on the organization and well-being of our future societies. The space occupied by economists in the media and academic institutions must be challenged as well, along with their disproportionate influence in the conduct of world affairs and university life, where it all begins.

In this context, one may inquire about whether the purpose of economics should be to serve society or whether the latter should concede to economics' authority. The current dominant discourse, which supports neoliberal policies, is based on the belief in the absolute efficiency of markets and a vision of economics as a mechanism obedient to natural laws, making economists for societies what physicists are for nature.

This credence that is shared in the academic world encourages individuals to pursue their own interests to generate maximum profits, and renders government or public intervention harmful to the economic well-being of a society. The absence of pluralism in the rationalization of economics erases, in this regard, the social and societal obligations of the collective entity and constitutes a potential threat to democracy.

In response to the recession of 2008, Mirowski lamented that the very neoliberal doctrinaires who had caused the crisis now called for a global drive for austerity measures and an end of government intervention that would further worsen the situation in countries such as Greece. Attending a meeting organized to discuss the state of affairs at the Institute for New Economic Thinking held at Bretton Woods in April 2011, he argued that instead of debating the failure of economist academics and the wreckage of economic thought and possible solutions, "many at the conference confessed their perplexity as 'the crisis is over but where was the fix?'"[10]

In presenting the economic reality as a product of market forces, a fact of nature against which no intervention was warranted, the dominant economic thinking imposed its views in an authoritarian fashion. Yet laissez-faire could not be the solution to a problem that affected millions. Considering the financial, social, and environmental costs it caused, the economic crisis demanded a reconceptualization of the systemic role and place of economics, both locally and globally, which never came to pass.

A historical analysis of storytelling and narratives about real-life experience can reveal how economic ideas affect collective choices and how they result from a concerted social, cultural, and political discourse. This analysis can inspire students to participate in socioeconomic debates and explore alternatives to mainstream economics. It can also encourage faculty to incorporate new cross-disciplinary pedagogical approaches that include, for example, the reading of literature to foster a broader and more informed reflection about the socioeconomic impasses and challenges of the twenty-first century.

HISTORICISM, NARRATIVE, EMPATHY

Three critical approaches reveal the impact literature can have on students majoring in economics (or any other field of study, for that matter). Through the concept of narrative imagination, Martha Nussbaum correlated the ability to be an intelligent reader of another person's story to the capacity for being a democratic and cultivated world citizen. Paulo Freire's concept of critical pedagogy asserted the political relevance of reading as a means of developing a consciousness of freedom, empowering the imagination, and raising the awareness of students so that they become subjects rather than objects. Drawing on psychology and narrative theory, Suzanne Keen more recently presented in *Empathy and the Novel* an account of the relationship between novel reading and altruism.

When he published *The Grapes of Wrath*, John Steinbeck was well aware of the revolutionary aspect of his novel. The media was unleashed against the book, then considered to be a communist pamphlet. It disparaged its vulgar style and apparent socialistic stands. The book was even banned in several California cities. Despite this opposition, however, it became a best seller.

A year later, when the book was adapted by John Ford in a film that received several Oscar nominations, Steinbeck was awarded the prestigious Pulitzer Prize before being awarded the Nobel Prize for literature in 1962. Geographically and socially typed, the story met worldwide success thanks to the images of John Ford who popularized it. Furthermore, the humanistic dimension of the literary work, its archetypal symbolism, and allusion to biblical myths contributed to making it a classic of American and world literature.

John Steinbeck was born in Salinas, California. He spent his youth in a rural valley producing fruits and vegetables and was from childhood influenced by agricultural rhythms and the beauties of nature. After graduating from high school, he studied biology at Stanford University from 1920 to 1925, while working on a ranch as a fruit picker.

Most of his novels attest to his experience working the land. They are set in the aftermath of the 1929 crisis. As the US economy saw its production capacity climb much higher than consumer demand, corporate profits collapsed to the extent that investors sought to liquidate the shares they owned. From "Black Thursday," October 24, to "Black Tuesday," October 29, the stock market lost 25 percent of its value, and the shockwave spread gradually to the global economy in an event that would mark the beginning of the Great Depression, the greatest economic crisis of the twentieth century.

These events led to a lasting crisis of confidence in regard to the stock market and banking system, which deeply affected consumption and investment. Corporate bankruptcies increased as a result of the financial difficulties, and unemployment rose tenfold between 1929 and 1933.

While the Great Depression raged, part of the Midwest was hit by dust storms. The agricultural heart of the United States, the Great Plains' crops were destroyed and the land eroded. Deprived of resources, their equipment and homes buried under layers of dust, ruined and starving farmers took to the road by the thousands toward California, and nearly three million people were forced to leave their land.

Beyond merely allowing a passive assimilation of historical facts, reading fosters students' active participation in considering and empathizing with other people's experience, rethinking, in this specific instance, their knowledge of the field of economics and the extent to which it is socially constructed, and—through a renewed awareness of history as resulting from a struggle for justice and democracy—reconceptualizing their role in society.

The title of the book originated from a suggestion made by Carol Steinbeck, the first wife of the author, who proposed it in reference to "The Battle Hymn of the Republic" by Julia Ward Howe, first published in *Atlantic Monthly* in 1862: "Mine eyes have seen the glory of the coming of the Lord: He is trampling out the vintage Where the grapes of wrath are Stored; He hath loosed the fateful lightning of His terrible swift sword. His truth is marching on."

These words evoke the return of the messiah and of divine justice that must one day deliver the world from the oppression of evil at the Last Judgment: "And another angel came out of the altar, which had power over fire; and cried with a loud cry to him that had a sharp sickle, saying, Thrust in thy sharp sickle, and gather the clusters of the vine of the earth, for her grapes are fully ripe" (Revelations 14:18).

The angel then launched its sickle to harvest the grapes of the earth, casting them into the winepress of the terrible wrath of God. The allusion to "the grapes of wrath" thus also referred to a biblical tradition that saw in the fruit of the vine the grapes of impiety and injustice. It denounced those who monopolized the goods of the earth and did not respect the divine law as in the Book of Nehemiah (13:1–52), and the allusion expresses God's discontent about those who were unfaithful to the covenant like in "The Parable of the Vineyard" (Isaiah 5:1–73).

At the same time, the trampled grapes pertain to the redemptive sacrifice of Christ who offers his blood for the forgiveness of sins. God's wrath is inseparable from his love for his creatures. Steinbeck associated his story with a secular hope of salvation and liberation. He gave voice through it to the unbearable cry of the poor, the captives who asked for deliverance through justice. Beyond the parable of the "suffering servant" in Isaiah, the novel bears witness to the blood of the oppressed that is flowing on the flag of rebellion, to the violence of injustice that inexorably drives the people to insurgency.

A passage in chapter 25 of the novel corroborates this interpretation: "And in the eyes of the hungry there is a growing wrath. In the souls of the people the grapes of wrath are filling and growing heavy, growing heavy for the vintage."[11] The Midwestern farmers found their land unworthy and dreamed of going westward where sweetness flows, to a "land flowing with milk and honey"—a reference that makes one think of the Book of Exodus.

Casy becomes the spiritual leader of the farmers, a modern figure of Moses once sent by God to free the Hebrews from the pharaoh's slavery. Similarly, the Joads, first among the farmers, escape from the iron hand of the banking empire and become aware of their status as elected people for the advent of a new order. Like the Hebrews, these migrants will find their "promised land."

Steinbeck teaches us that economics is not a self-sufficient field of study that mathematicians alone will help us comprehend. His symbolic and parabolic reading of the events caused by the 1929 crisis demonstrate that economics can indeed have social, biblical, existential, and democratic implications. Approached from these perspectives, it also enables students to understand the discipline from other viewpoints such as green theory or cross-cultural theory.

The whole story is based on a form of social messianism. The symbolism and biblical references confer to the novel a sense of timelessness and universality. But the story simultaneously presents a demystification of the biblical references that seem able to describe to the fullest extent the scandalous destitution and exploitation of the peasant masses living in a miserable and hopeless state of despair.

The land belongs to a few owners, large companies, or banks, whose sole purpose is to earn large profits. They represent the world of "fingers with soft flesh" that is not engaged in manual labor or confronted to its reality, a cold world, remote and unforgiving, that only obeys to the laws of "mathematics": "Some of them hated the mathematics that drove them, and some were afraid, and some worshiped the mathematics because it provided a refuge from thought and from feelings [. . .] Soft fingers began to tap the sill of the car window, and hard fingers tightened on the restless drawing sticks."[12]

Drought and dust storms only sped up the scheduled eviction of farmers. Land consolidation allowed mechanization and the division of the number of farmers by "twelve to fifteen" fold. This short-term financial logic exacerbated the economic downturn, causing massive unemployment. It led to an ecological catastrophe as monoculture depleted the soil and contributed to desertification and the subsequent dust storms.

Steinbeck condemned the crime perpetrated against Mother Earth by the depraved spirit of the banking system. He denounced the fate of tractors abandoned to themselves, and the "orgasms set by gears, raping methodically, raping without passion."[13] The resulting harvest was no longer human made: "The land bore under iron, and under iron gradually died; for it was not loved or hated, it had no prayers or curses."[14]

The soil now gave birth to a humanitarian tragedy through the impoverishment of families and farmers. Steinbeck describes the enormity of the inhumane conditions: "The man sitting in the iron seat did not look like a man; gloved, goggled, rubber dust mask over nose and mouth, he was a part of the monster, a robot in the seat . . . the driver's hands could not twitch because the monster that built the tractor, the monster that sent the tractor out, had somehow got into the driver's hands, into his brain and muscle, had goggled him and muzzled him."[15]

The biologist, the seasonal worker, and the poet in Steinbeck found that Earth now submitted to the laws of a new destructive order. He fostered through the story an ecological conscience. If farmers recognized their responsibility in monocultures, capitalism, for its part, was ultimately responsible for imposing its law on an exhausted land and people.

The novel also alludes to the tragedy of forced economic migration still affecting millions around the world today. The farmers' expulsions tear apart their roots: "Place where folks live is them folks. They ain't whole, out lonely on the road in a piled-up car. They ain't alive no more."[16] The actions taken by anonymous companies prejudiced humanity by destroying its emotional memory, the expertise and know-how of the community: "So easy that the wonder goes out of work, so efficient that the wonder goes out of the land and the working of it, and with the wonder the deep understanding and the relation."[17]

With the population's displacement, it is the social and societal fabric of the nation that is affected. Steinbeck shows in chapter 13 how the gas station attendants and the general convenience stores were the first victims of the departure of peasants. Early on, the reader sees how the labor force weighs little against the omnipotence of capital that uses the constraint of the law to evict the farmers. When those who are expelled take the road, they cannot conform to the laws and formalities of a transformed society.

From a social perspective, Steinbeck recognized that humans were "political animals." He did not find the moral existence of society on any sacred ground but on the necessity to cohabit in order to ensure the group's survival. In this sense, he used the principles of anthropological functionalism of Herbert Spencer and extended the positivist sociological morality of Emile Durkheim, who asserted that societies could only reconcile order and freedom through the proper division of labor.

Threatening the social order, the expulsion of farmers puts the very existence of society in peril. Steinbeck prophesies that, driven to despair by injustice and the blind laws of the market, their violence would spread against the capitalist process of exclusion: "Everyone is a drum major leading a parade of hurts, marching with our bitterness. And some day—the armies of bitterness will all be going the same way. And they'll all walk together, and there'll be a dead terror from it."[18]

Criticizing the absurd, inhuman logic of economic policy, Steinbeck reveals the existence of a "promised land" that could not feed its population despite the abundance of crops. Describing starving children while piles of fruits, vegetables, and meat were forbidden for consumption, he condemns a form of savage capitalism driven by selfishness, shamelessly hiding behind the avid search for maximum profit. While the purchasing power of the common people collapsed, production no longer found creditworthy consumers. Rather than seeing the market collapse further, the big landowners preferred destroying their surplus and forcing the bankruptcy of small farms.

Reflecting Paulo Freire's critical pedagogy, Jim Casy, a traveling preacher, seeks to educate Tom Joad, the main character, by awakening his class consciousness and desire for the common good. Having experienced the power of words in his sermons, Casy now refuses to use them to enslave his flock, condemning the hypocrisy of economically driven societies with a language understandable to people: "Gonna cuss an' swear an' hear the poetry of folks talkin'."[19]

The emancipation of the poor implies here a liberation from the forces of religious authorities. Beyond moralistic figures of speech, union representatives and political advocates substitute the notions of just and unjust for those of good and evil.

Like Émile Zola, Steinbeck was the novelist of poverty. Like his predecessor, his novel gave a journalistic testimony of socialist humanism. He also expanded his message through an archetypal symbolism that drew on the Bible, even if the mystical aura of the sacred book was ultimately reduced to an earthly horizon. His visceral attachment to Mother Earth and quest for a paradise lost was demonstrated by the manner in which he portrayed the tragic events of the period.

Yet out of the people's miserable experiences also emerged a solidarity and generosity among common people that offered them hope. The massive, desperate rural-to-urban migration could have taken place in the midst of general indifference and ignorance. However, provoking much public reaction, Steinbeck alerted readers to the harmful, deadly consequences of laissez-faire economics on the human condition and for the well-being of society.

He exposed the economic mechanisms at the time that brought the peasants on the roads: an increased agricultural mechanization and productivity that substantially reduced the demand of the labor force. His focus on the structural causes of social inequality, and the uncontrolled and irrational effects of unbridled capitalism, revealed how an oppressed humankind could easily become an ordinary commodity, a tool at the service and mercy of profit making.

The story could be used in this respect as an introduction to cross-cultural issues pertaining to economic theory and reality through the comparative reading of Hispanic narrative fiction such as *Una Carta a Dios* by Gregorio López y Fuentes and *Un Día de estos* by Gabriel García Márquez, for example, and works by Charles Dickens or John Dos Passos. Literary narrative and critical pedagogy should be required reading for economic students because of the political and empathic relevance of reading such texts.

Many circumstances today expose the extent to which the mercantile and utilitarian dimension of economics is at the core of human tragedies worldwide. From India to Kenya, Romania to Colombia, farmers keep intact a generosity that enables them to preserve their dignity, and to survive the global collusion between money and power. Their earthy common sense and determination lead them to regroup and help them to survive.

Calling for the solidarity of all farmers and workers in society, *The Grapes of Wrath*, among others, needs to be included in the curriculum of economics majors. It will broaden their awareness of the farmer and proletariat conditions worldwide, particularly in poor and developed countries, and the deadly consequences that economists' decisions have on people.

As such, Steinbeck's novel remains a work relevant to our time. Globalization and unbridled capitalism continue to cause natural disasters; a few rich countries confiscate the majority of the world's natural resources; large companies monopolize agricultural productions to the detriment of small farmers; entire populations are abandoned on the roads of their exodus; workers and children are still exploited for miserable wages; and mafias weave secret ties with political power to develop new forms of human traf-ficking and slavery.

Steinbeck attested to the only path of hope that may lead us beyond the grapes of wrath, that of a rational sharing of resources and wealth. Through his work, literature and the humanities unveil the concerns and sufferings of humankind like no other academic fields ever could. They uncover the grave consequences economic policy can have on millions and the crucial urgency of humanizing economic pedagogy today.

QUESTIONING *HOMO ECONOMICUS*

Following the 2006 to 2007 subprime mortgage crisis, the financial and economic downturn of 2008 affected most of the industrialized countries and is considered the worst to have occurred since the Great Depression. It was marked by a shortage of confidence that quickly affected the stock markets. It led to falling prices and a credit crunch for both companies and house-holds, ultimately weighing on global economic activity. The banking crisis began when several US financial institutions became insolvent and had to either be saved by the US Federal Reserve, such as the insurance company AIG, or liquidated, such as Lehman Brothers, along with people's invest-ments.

The American economy was the first to enter into recession followed by the Eurozone and the rest of the world. Governments and central banks reacted in a concerted effort to avoid the bankruptcy of large banks and come to the rescue of financial institutions that were "too big to fail." To this end, the US government (taxpayers) took over some of the toxic assets held by private banks to bail them out.

The rescue of financial institutions caused public debt to rise further (it has now reached seventeen trillion in the United States), along with the fear of the risk of new financial bubbles to burst. Meanwhile, the situation in countries such as Greece required the rapid implementation of austerity measures through tax increases and public spending cuts that accentuated even further the rise of poverty and unemployment.

What could this event reveal about the importance of the humanities? First, they are in no way responsible for what constitutes a real threat to the future of democracy and peace in the world. Second, the crisis—which caused a significant increase in social inequalities and the bankruptcy of Western governments—should challenge and call into question the pedagog-ical methods of economics instruction.

Third, a reconceptualization of the teaching of this discipline must in-volve liberal arts approaches, such as genuine critical thinking and the use of narrative imagination. Fourth, a failure to reconsider the tenets of economics in higher education will aggravate the tension already palpable between the political establishment and the people's democratic aspirations.

It is revelatory that the constraints of budget deficits reduction emanating from institutions such as the IMF and the World Bank, for example, have repeatedly bypassed democratic suffrage to the point where, under the pressure of unelected bodies, heads of States in Greece and Italy were replaced by technocrats designated to implement IMF directives.

The 2008 economic recession has weakened the social contract on which democracy was founded. This situation raises the specter of the 1930s during which the excesses of unbridled financial capitalism and the limited role of public policy and institutions led political governance to fall into the hands of totalitarian regimes.

It is worth noting also that the United States preserved its parliamentary system during that period via the New Deal, conceived through the intellectual contributions and political involvements of academics such as John Rogers Commons and John Dewey. The two envisioned a project through which the social sciences and liberal arts would play a role in the preservation and enhancement of democracy.

Both promoted the increased participation of individuals in the public governance of society to assert a greater democratic control of financial and industrial powers and enhanced a collective purpose to the economy and corporate accountability. Confronted with the rise of fascism and nazism in Europe, Dewey opposed a spirit of cooperation in society and called for the emergence of a "creative democracy" that would enhance moral forces in social institutions and the implementation of economic policy.

The recent financial crisis also revealed a striking opposition between two different approaches of envisioning citizens' relationship to economics: it suggests on the one hand that the hypothetical *homo economicus* is a subject mainly interested in the accumulation of wealth and the maximization of profit, while, on the other, the *homo reciprocans* privileges collective cooperation.

Each conception is rooted in the eighteenth and nineteenth century and offers different perspectives on the socioeconomic role of individuals in society. John Stuart Mill contended in *Essays on Some Unsettled Questions of Political Economy* that each citizen's main concern should be to possess wealth and assess the means for gaining it by obtaining the greatest amount of necessities, conveniences, and luxuries, with the smallest quantity of labor.

Adam Smith similarly alleged in *The Wealth of Nations* that humans were above all self-interested beings; yet he had declared a few years earlier in *The Theory of Moral Sentiments* that they should have sympathy for the well-being of others. Aristotle's *Politics* already highlighted the limits and dangers of selfishness, in stark contrast to the great pleasure of performing a kindness or service to friends, guests, or companions.

The concept of *homo economicus*, on which business models are conceived today according to market efficiency and the maximizing of individual usefulness and welfare, has been undermined by Pierre Bourdieu among others in *The Social Structure of the Economy*. His main criticisms concerned the fact that economic theories were based on rational behavioral assumptions. As a branch of the social sciences, Bourdieu argued, economics could not function independently from the legal, political, and cultural domains. Those who made of the *homo economicus* a universal being did not sufficiently account for the specificities of each individual social milieu.

According to this view, economists uncritically accepted concepts such as "market," "growth," or "demands" without taking the full measure of their historical dimension. Hyper-rational and driven exclusively by the coldness of calculation, the neoclassical *homo economicus* possessed a presumed logic and rationale that economists alone could masterfully analyze and evaluate through mathematic means.

Bourdieu should be included in the reading list of students in economics to the extent that he attempts to bring the latter academic field under the fold of history and human experience, arguing that any behavior or practice should be approached from a social and societal perspective.

He outlined in that regard a set of principles that challenge the prerogatives of economics as a domain of inquiry in higher education. First, the social world encompasses every economic action; second, economic science is the product of history; third, *homo economicus* can best be apprehended through the notion of "habitus" (among them acquired sensibilities and tastes); and fourth, economic paradigms such as need or propensities are not endogenous (having an internal cause or origin) but exogenous.

Each point alludes to the notion that economics as an academic discipline is socially constructed, social space being defined as a field of struggle within which individuals occupy different positions determined by the amount of capital they have accumulated during their life. Contrary to what was alleged in neoclassical theories, the market was not the result of a simple rational encounter between supply and demand based exclusively on an economic calculation.

While the modern world of *homo economicus* exalted competition and egotism penetrated the minds of economists, Bourdieu argued for a greater cooperation to counter the phenomenon of economic marginalization and exploitation.

Beyond the consumerist impulse of greed, he maintained that college students should respond to the moral and ethical considerations social science and liberal education presented so that the *homo politicus* should prevail over the *economicus*.

Through critical instruction, it was in his view the responsibility of society to protect us against the decline of citizenship. Exalting rivalry and struggle in the conquest for "extrinsic goods" such as material wealth and social status, the pursuit of happiness also required the need for "sympathy" as Adam Smith used the term in his *Theory of Moral Sentiments*.

The definition and conception one gives of *homo economicus* in the classroom and beyond thus has profound political implications. Freed from the constraints of the Old Regime, Alexis de Tocqueville noted that liberal societies imposed increased competition that could be detrimental to democracy "when all the prerogatives of birth and fortune [were] destroyed, and all professions [were] open to everyone ambitious."[20]

Yet the vision of *homo economicus* as greedy, emotionless, and socially disengaged does not take into account that individuals are also inherently *homo ethicus* and *empathicus* and that their economic decisions are not necessarily driven by the search for maximum profit.

It is this latter facet of humankind that the humanities alone are capable of nurturing in undergraduates and graduates of economic programs. We have seen how approached as a mathematical model, the "economic man" is dehumanized and only responsive to consumerist impulses deeply inscribed in the globalized economy.

Pedagogical approaches to teaching economics that include political, critical, and cultural theory, feminism, and psychoanalysis will significantly broaden the students' understanding of their field on pressing issues of our time, including globalization, economic ends, equality, and the marketization of society, and meaningfully rehumanize their grasp of the subject.

Joseph Stiglitz has shown in *The Price of Inequality* and more recently *The Great Divide* how inequality of income and wealth have increased with the financialization of the economy. More fundamentally, the threat of climate change and financial instability is a daily reminder of the planetary confinement of globalization, and finite natural resources are exploited at times to their limits while the basic needs of populations worldwide remain unsatisfied.

The creative and critical dimensions of the humanities are essential in this context because they can call into question the systems of knowledge and analyses at play in socioeconomics. Jean-François Lyotard's concept of "libidinal economy" demonstrated the importance of critical thinking and intellectual pondering on these issues. It revealed how hidden unconscious forces under the guise of rationality often determined society's political economy.

To fully consider this concealment in economics teaching and research and its social and societal ramifications, students need to question from a liberal arts perspective the philosophy of the subject, the process of signification, and the foundation of language. According to Lyotard, libinal energy constitutes one of the main driving forces of any "theoretical fiction" and the foundation of any given economic system, rationalization, explanation, and justification.

Rejecting any totalizing approaches to the subject, Lyotard attempted to explore how different forces and forms of desire were at work in local and global economics. *Libidinal economy* marked his political break with revolutionary Marxism, giving a more libertarian and hedonistic account of desire and pleasure in the public and economic policy of capitalist societies.

Remaining faithful to the political exigency he valued most—honesty and justice, but also the singularities of individuals that made them heterogeneous and immeasurable—he questioned what was taken for granted (e.g., the reliability of logic, reason, representation, and interpretation) and in so doing reassessed the significance of nonrational forces in society.

What drove economic policy and transformed society thus rested as much on preconceived structures and concepts as on the idiosyncrasies of libidinal energy. As importantly, the dislocation of grand narratives underscored for Lyotard the equivocal nature of all scientific beliefs and the limits of any rational economic discourse.

Seeking to elaborate a more gender-inclusive economics, feminists have pointed out, for their part, how the models and methods of mainstream economics are biased toward the masculine. Julie Nelson argued in this respect that the field of study has been largely analyzed and understood through a logic that is masculine and therefore abstract and exclusive, while a feminine approach of the discipline would emphasize practicality and inclusion.

Feminists also challenged the notion that economics was a positive science, contending that the issues economists studied and debated resulted from a belief system that was influenced by various ideological, cultural, or social factors. In this respect, economic research was founded on constructed narratives resulting from power relations.

From feminist economists' approach, the male-dominated view explained why women were put at a disadvantage in Western and non-Western societies. In line with Amartya Sen, they contended that gender and race, as well as the social conditioning of citizens, should be taken into account in economic analysis given that "the systematically inferior position of women inside and outside the household in many societies point[ed] to the necessity of treating gender as a force of its own in development analysis."[21]

Similarly, Bipasha Baruah investigated "the continuing importance and implications of issues of redistribution and to demonstrate their interconnection with issues of recognition."[22]

Both libidinal and feminist approaches to economics have major pedagogical ramifications that pertain both to course content and to students' perceptions of the field of study. They also concern the preponderant question of the relation between knowledge and power, specifically how theories, norms, and values are constructed, introduced to, and acquired by the future participants and decision makers of society.

Condemning the marketization of American universities and how "market fundamentalism" was jeopardizing democratic values, Henry Giroux has argued that the quest for profits and market-driven forces in the curriculum endangered the social contract between people and their leaders, ran opposite to the common good, and "reduced the obligations of citizenship to the act of consuming."[23]

He analyzed how the pedagogical methods used in the teaching of economics combined with the financial situation of the United States contributed to the making of a society in grave decline, focusing his attention in *America's Education and the Crisis of Public Values* on the treatment of youth. Far from promoting civic and democratic participation, the prevailing educational system inclined individuals toward careerism and consumerism as the only horizon of existence, which according to Giroux revealed a steady move away from and abandonment of its original humanistic core values.

Beyond the ivory tower, any violent and authoritarian political regime was not independent of a socioeconomic and cultural context that made possible the germination of such a governance. The emergence of a system practicing a form of Casino Capitalism engendered the domination of the wealthy, who increased their power through an antisocial platform.

Lacking information and deprived of critical ability on the subject, a majority of the American public, including millions of students in higher education, were led to believe in the infallibility of market-driven societies and in the necessity to cut welfare expenditure, while the federal government spent $700 billion a year for its military budget, an amount spent on militaries worldwide.

In this context, the fostering of critical literary and cultural theory and the rise of consciousness through narrative imagination could enable students in economics to challenge the status quo and formulate methods of criticism that appraise the questioning of accepted knowledge and authority pertaining to given norms and values.

Through a new pedagogy asserting the importance of ethics and of responsibility toward others, "Darwinian Casino Capitalism [could] be resisted and defeated by instilling in students an ability for independent thinking, and a passion for the freedom of speech and critical analysis."[24]

GLOBALIZATION WITH A HUMAN FACE

With the rise of financial globalization and welfare corporatism, state regulations have been reduced to enabling private investors to borrow directly on the financial markets. Disconnected from the reality of earning and production, a new virtual economy emerged in which banks, companies, and shareholders seek through speculation an ever-faster return on short-term investment.

The end of the Cold War created the illusion that, along with the emergence of a new world order, capitalism and democracy had triumphed globally. As Francis Fukuyama proclaimed the "end of history," rich countries began to benefit from economic globalization. A wider range of goods was accessible globally at a lower price, and shareholders received a better return on their investment as factories outsourced their production to poorer countries.

Ultimately economics majors need to have a better understanding of what a twenty-first-century "globalization with a human face" may look like. In *Globalization and Its Discontents*, Joseph Stiglitz contended that unlike wealthy nations, the poorest countries did not benefit from the outcome of globalization. Their main economic resource, agriculture, was in fact undermined by the protectionist policies of rich countries, a support that increased inequalities between the richest and the poorest on the planet.

Globalization from an economic perspective is not only blind to the suffering of people but dependent upon it. According to a report from Amnesty International, major technology companies buy electronic components made from minerals mined by children as young as seven. Collecting, sorting, and cleaning mineral ores, these children expose themselves to particles that lead to lung-related illnesses.

Unbeknown to most technology users, a 2014 estimate by UNICEF put the number of children working in southern Democratic Republic of Congo mines at about forty thousand. Those who work in cobalt mines make between $1 and $2 a day, according to the report: "Many of [the Big Tech] companies stated that they have a zero tolerance policy when it comes to child labor in their supply chains. However, they did not provide details of specific investigations and checks that they have undertaken to identify and address child labor in their cobalt supply chains."

In the words of Stiglitz, recipient of the Nobel Prize for economics in 2001, globalization lay entirely on neoliberalism and "market fundamentalism." Instead of allowing poor countries to lift themselves out of poverty, it tended to serve the interests of Western and Northern nations. Moving wealth and resources from poor to rich countries, globalization favored the large financial and industrial interests at the expense of citizens, he argued.

Born through the Bretton Woods agreements in July 1944, the current mission of the International Monetary Fund neither corresponded with the original aspirations of its founders (among them John Maynard Keynes), nor reached any of its objectives set at the time: financial stability and the eradication or significant reduction of poverty. This failure, according to Stiglitz, was explained by the fact that the international stage is dominated by developed countries, multinational companies, and major banks that follow their own interests.

As of 2012, 12.7 percent of the world's population lived at or below $1.90 a day, and over 2.1 billion people in the developing world lived on less than $3.10 a day.[25] As stated by the UN Millennium Development Goals Report of 2015, nearly half of all deaths in children under age five were attributed to malnutrition, and an estimated 825 million people still lived in extreme poverty and suffered from hunger.

Far from being limited to the realm of economics, globalization with a human face should encompass the valorization of the political, cultural, and human rights domains. Beyond the scope of speculation and capital investment, it should focus on the needs of all citizens worldwide: access to food and water, education, health care, and the responsible pursuit of life and happiness. It ought to be a political project that works toward the integration of all people in their societies.

Remarkably absent from any introductory- or intermediate-level book on macroeconomics, Stiglitz questioned a highly dehumanized globalization ruled by the presumed self-regulatory powers of the market that favored the rich nations at the expense of the poor. Also notably absent is Amartya Sen, who highlighted the need to explore the relation between democracy and economic development, and the role of the state in the redistribution of wealth from an ethical perspective.

Based on real-life experience, the latter argued in *Poverty and Famines: An Essay on Entitlement and Deprivation* that the Bengal famine of 1943—during which three million people died—was due not only to a lack of food but also to the inequalities caused by the failure of distribution mechanisms. Sen later concluded that this disaster should have been avoided, production having been higher than in previous years: "In order to understand starvation, it [was] necessary to go into the structure of ownership."[26]

Lessons from such disastrous policies should be analyzed by students as much as Mohandas Karamchand Gandhi's views on ethics, inequality, altruism, and charity, and the limitations of wants. According to Sen, economics is a moral science rather than a mathematical science. Known for his insightful work on inequality worldwide and as the heir to Bengali humanism, Sen founded his theses on his reading of Adam Smith's *The Theory of Moral Sentiments*.

Economics majors need to distance themselves from their own immediate interests and imagine being in the place of the less fortunate. This reciprocal compassion is only achievable through a mutual knowledge and understanding of others that makes living in common possible.

Beyond their scientific and mathematical pretentions, future economists should recognize that their field continuously requires moral considerations: "Not only was the so-called 'father of modern economics,' Adam Smith, a

Professor of Moral Philosophy at the University of Glasgow . . . but the subject of economics was for a long time seen as something like a branch of ethics."[27]

Economic policy cannot be dissociated from moral sentiments such as sympathy, compassion, and solidarity. A positivist and scientific approach to economics impoverishes considerably the scope of the academic discipline. Adam Smith based his initial research on the observation of poverty and the role of ethical considerations in human behavior.

In light of this contract that transcends historical periods, one of the major deficiencies of contemporary economic theory today is that it narrows the broad vision economists should have of human experience, such as the humanities' novel (storytelling), ethics, and cultural study.

This is particularly revealing when exploring issues pertaining to the link between inequality, social justice, and the environment, including pollution and the depletion of natural resources provoked by economic development. Human activities have had a considerable impact on biodiversity, and therefore on the future of all living species.

The "economics" of the environment revealed a dramatic, alarming situation of our biosphere. The current rate of species extinction is one hundred to one thousand times greater than what it was in the history of the evolution of the planet. In 2007, the International Union for the Conservation of Nature assessed that the survival of one in eight bird species, one in four mammalian species, one in three amphibian species, and 70 percent of all plants was endangered.

Globalization with a human face demands that students be introduced to the consequences and limits of economic growth and development, a crucial issue also absent in college manuals. The cause of the massive extinction of species is mainly human made, especially since the Industrial Revolution during which human activity increased considerably. Unlimited growth leads to the degradation of natural habitat, the pollution of water and soil, as well as climate change.

The World Wildlife Fund's Living Planet Report 2014 stated that "more than 10,000 representative populations of mammals, birds, reptiles, amphibians, and fish" have dropped by 52 percent since 1970. This means that "in less than two human generations, populations sizes of vertebrate species have dropped by half."[28]

Never in the history of the world has a species dominated all others to the point where it can affect their very existence. Students should learn in this context how sustainable development must fulfill the needs of the present without compromising the life of future generations. Donella H. Meadows, Jorgen Randers, and Dennis L. Meadows discussed the urgency of reducing economic needs to meet the capacity of the planet.[29]

The current economic and financial systems place impossible demands upon finite earth resources. How can we conceive under the circumstances that no Green Party has been able to access the American political platform in what is considered the most important democracy in the world?

Students should partake in the debate between environmental economics who apply tools of economics to address environmental problems, and ecological economists who consider that economics is a subfield of ecology. While the former argue that natural capital can be substituted by human-made capital and market laws, the latter promote an economy that functions as a subsystem of the ecosystem and aims at preserving natural capital.

Liberal education can play an as-yet-unrecognized central role in this debate by raising new perspectives on economic and environmental issues as attested by the critical approaches that have recently emerged in the humanities—such as ecofeminism, postcolonial ecojustice, posthumanism, and green theory. These approaches enable students to learn about the poor and disenfranchised around the world and provide critical information that is far more inclusive, humanly speaking, than the narrow scope of pure economics.

Economics majors must also be introduced to the work of Hans Jonas, who argued in *The Imperative of Responsibility* that the economic model of the West was not viable in the long term if it did not become more aware of its impact on the environment. They must rethink their role as citizens and cosignatories of a contract acknowledging their obligation toward the natural world.

Students must also be given the opportunity to explore the content of André Comte-Sponville's seminal book *Le capitalisme est-il moral?* (*Is Capitalism Moral?*) and the interrelation among economic, social, cultural, and environmental domains. Whether it concerns eradicating poverty or safeguarding the future of our planet, authors, advocates, critical thinkers, and theorists from different geographic horizons constitute essential sources for economists who wish to rethink their field's boundaries.

As world citizens, they should be aware of the Millennium Development Goals set in 2000 under the auspices of the United Nations, among them reducing extreme poverty and child mortality; combatting epidemics; promoting education of minorities, gender equality, and the empowerment of women; and implementing sustainable development.

Why do we educate and what purpose do we assign the social sciences and the humanities through this process? Our ultimate aspirations when teaching and/or conducting research in the liberal arts should be none other than making the world a better place—that is to say, from an economic perspective, more egalitarian and attentive to the plight of the human condition worldwide and to its environment.

Louis Menand rightly cautioned that "in a society that encourages its members to pursue the career paths that promise the greatest personal or financial rewards, people will, given a choice, learn only what they need to know for success. They will have no incentive to acquire the knowledge and skills important for life as an informed citizen."[30] Humanizing economics contributes to rebuilding the bridge between the university and society and demonstrating how the societal and existential worth of the humanities are more valuable than mere economic and technological assessments can indicate.

NOTES

1. Michael Bérubé, "How We Got Here," Presidential Address, *Publication of the Modern Language Association of America* 128, no. 3 (2013): 531.

2. Bérubé, "How We Got Here," 536.

3. Joshua Clover, "Value, Theory, Crisis," *PMLA* 127, no. 1 (2012): 107.

4. Michael DeWilde, "The Business of the Humanities," *Chronicle of Higher Education*, July 1, 2005.

5. John Maynard Keynes, *The General Theory of Employment, Interest and Money* (Cambridge: MacMillan, 1936), 297.

6. UN Human Development Report 2001.

7. "Richest 1% Will Own More Than All the Rest by 2016," *Oxfam America*, January 19, 2015, https://www.oxfam.org/en/pressroom/pressreleases/2015-01-19/richest-1-will-own-more-all-rest-2016.

8. Joseph A. Schumpeter, *History of Economic Analysis* (Oxford: Oxford University Press, 1996), 4.

9. Keynes, *The General Theory of Employment, Interest and Money*, 383–84.

10. Philip Mirowski, *Never Let a Serious Crisis Go to Waste: How Neoliberalism Survived the Financial Meltdown* (New York: Verso, 2014), 5.

11. John Steinbeck, *The Grapes of Wrath* (New York: Alfred A. Knopf, Inc., 1993), 445.

12. Steinbeck, *The Grapes of Wrath*, 38, 40.

13. Steinbeck, *The Grapes of Wrath*, 44.

14. Steinbeck, *The Grapes of Wrath*, 45.

15. Steinbeck, *The Grapes of Wrath*, 43–44.

16. Steinbeck, *The Grapes of Wrath*, 65.

17. Steinbeck, *The Grapes of Wrath*, 147.

18. Steinbeck, *The Grapes of Wrath*, 111.

19. Steinbeck, *The Grapes of Wrath*, 119.

20. Alexis de Toqueville, "Why Americans Seem So Restless in the Midst of Their Well-Being," *Democracy in America*, Volume II, Chapter 13 (New York: The Library of America, 2004), 627.

21. Amartya Sen, "Gender and Cooperative Conflicts," in Irene Tinker, ed., *Persistent Inequalities: Women and World Development* (New York: Oxford University Press, 1990), 123.

22. Bipasha Baruah, *Women and Property in Urban India* (Vancouver: UBC Press, 2010), 8.

23. Henry Giroux, *Education and the Crisis of Public Values* (New York: Peter Lang, 2011), 51.

24. Henry A. Giroux, *Zombie Politics and Culture in the Age of Casino Capitalism* (New York: Peter Lang, 2010), 21.

25. World Bank Report, October 7, 2015.

26. Amartya Sen, *Poverty and Famines: An Essay on Entitlement and Deprivation* (Oxford: Oxford University Press, 1983), 1.

27. Amartya Sen, *On Ethics and Economics* (Malden, MA: Blackwell Publishing, 1987), 2.

28. "World Wildlife Fund Global," *World Wildlife Fund for Nature*, 2016, http://wwf. panda.org/.

29. Donella H. Meadows, Jorgen Randers, and Dennis L. Meadows, *Limits to Growth: The 30-Year Update* (Burlington, VT: Chelsea Green Publishing, 2004).

30. Louis Menand, "Live and Learn: Why We Have College," *The New Yorker*, June 6, 2011.

Chapter Three

Searching for STEM's *Telos*

In an address delivered at Cambridge University in 1882 known as the Rede Lecture and titled "Literature and Science," Matthew Arnold criticized those such as Thomas Huxley, who were remonstrating against the predominance of letters in education, regarding *belles lettres* as mere superficial humanism, and situating them in opposition to positive science or what they considered to be true knowledge.

At a time when the college curriculum centered on classical literature, Matthew Arnold and Thomas Huxley debated in the latter nineteenth century whether academic programs should also include the natural sciences. Huxley's view that science should be included in the curriculum would ultimately prevail, alongside of the notion that any educated person at a university should be informed and learn from the new discoveries of scientific inquiry.

While the Victorian period, marked by the Industrial Revolution, was affecting and transforming the lives of many, Arnold favored an education that focused on literature, philosophy, and the arts that contrasted substantially with Huxley's opinion, presented in *Science and Culture*, that the knowledge of most worth was technical and scientific.

In many ways, the Arnold-Huxley debate is still relevant to our times. New generations are immersed more than ever before in high-tech/smartphone-driven societies. As the college curriculum reveals, the number of courses that require technological literacy such as STS ("Science and Technology in Society") has dramatically increased. Furthermore, universities seek to respond to the urge of economic competition by offering more courses geared toward the acquisition of mathematic and scientific knowledge while teaching and research in the liberal arts has been steadily challenged and undermined.

THE LIMITS OF SCIENCE

Even as early as the 1800s, Thomas Huxley believed that a comprehensive scientific education was needed to enhance individual lives and achieve industrial progress. From his point of view, the advancement of law, medicine, and economics demanded the promotion of social and physical science education, and students engaged in these critical and strategic disciplines did not need to receive a classical education.

In contrast, Arnold contended that the emphasis on modern science and technology was compromising the ideals of truth and beauty (problematic ideals, even from a humanities standpoint). It was furthermore undermining the search for human aspiration and achievement through morals, ethics, and wisdom. In this light, the importance of literary education prevailed over the natural sciences that omitted what was most essential in human nature: the intimate knowledge of self and the world through the conduit of aesthetics and the intellect.

Arnold's reflections sought to underscore the limits of science in its ambition to provide a systematic knowledge of the physical and natural world through observation and experimentation. Could an objective understanding and explanation of nature be truly achieved? The limits of science were revealed through the reliability or unreliability of the scientist's observation, and thus the human capacity to inquire and answer questions about phenomena.

In spite of its overwhelming achievements in areas such as communication, medicine, transportation, or the environment, the realm of science is not limitless. It can help humanity describe how the world is, but it does not make moral judgments about, for example, euthanasia or human and animal rights. It can uncover the frequency of a sound and how the eye relays information to the brain, but it does not recognize beauty.

Many consider this lack of moral and aesthetic judgment crucial in scientific study, but, as we will suggest, the assumption of objectivity can actually have a negative impact on scientific study, as well as on culture in general.

Perhaps more importantly, it is not the purview of science to explain how to make ethical use of scientific knowledge. It does not indicate whether the recombination of DNA should be used to remedy genetic disease. This decision falls outside its bounds. Finally, science does not derive conclusions about metaphysical inquiries falling beyond the realm of nature. Yet these questions relative to moral and aesthetic judgments, ethics and philosophy, are subjects of scholarly investigations, and they greatly influence human societies and actions.

The limits of science thus call for a reflection about its end and means. First, not all inquiries central to the human experience are answerable through science. Second, when science contributes to the construction of knowledge about the natural world, this knowledge is dynamic and relative to a geographic milieu and a historical context. Third, its assumptions or deductions are revisable and lead to new unanswered questions.

Fourth, the assumption that science necessarily results from the relation between thought and reality poses another problem: do facts exist outside of thought and emerge from the natural phenomena, or do phenomena pertain to the human mind's construction that can be analyzed through psychological, physiological, sociological, and/or historical perspectives?

An essential issue resides in knowing how or to what extent the mind appropriates and integrates data into a discourse, or whether it creates it, making it fictive and/or subjective, and thus unscientific. Resulting from gathering proofs and evidences, should science solely involve a passive collection or demand a reflection about the genuine nature of its findings?

In order to reach any sort of conclusion on the subject, one must acknowledge that science requires one to trust what is given, which, as it were, has the last word for scientists who cannot contradict "factual" evidence. But this faithfulness or trust does not simply entail an observation without trials.

One cannot explore scientific knowledge without considering its epistemological dimension, yet science education routinely demands that we do just this. Also typically left undiscussed is what defines the specificity of the methodological approaches of science in relation to other types of discourse.

Auguste Comte's positivism stipulated that science should gather facts with the greatest neutrality possible, without making assumptions or extrapolations that might introduce an element of subjectivity. Science must therefore be faithful to the object and wary of what subjectivity adds to it. It must be distinguished from faith and opinion and construct a discourse that is as much as possible consistent with the nature of the object.

However, things are more complicated if one considers that the mind sorts and selects the facts and constructs their representations and narratives. Science must remain as close as possible to the real, but it cannot be content with observing and recording facts. The mind classifies and puts them in order. It organizes them through the faculties of the analyst or translator. Interpreting and giving meaning to the data found in nature, the subjective mind filters our relation to and determines reality.

At the same time, a neutral observation, devoid of any active work of the mind, would be sterile, a shapeless mass of facts that could not give access to true knowledge. What science can seek in that regard is concepts to unite essential features of objective phenomenon. It discovers patterns and assigns categories, allowing one to predict, provoke, prevent, or—as Descartes wrote in the *Discourse on Method*—"to make one the master and possessor of nature."[1]

The fact that the subjective is central to perceiving and knowing constitutes a challenge for science. How might one construct knowledge without creating fiction or arbitrary assumptions? The tradition of relativism, as promoted by the Sophists and skeptics of antiquity such as Pyrrho of Elis, postulates the ultimate impossibility of science due to the unfeasibility of impartial observation or, for that matter, ascertaining truth.

If one does not believe objective truth possible, one must suspend his or her judgments to avoid being deceived. It is impossible to prove that the skeptics are wrong, but skeptics themselves cannot prove that they are right. It would be contradictory to their own philosophy.

A narrow but fertile path is to accept that the concept of scientific "truth" is too ambitious and impractical. Kant critiqued the faculty of reason, and Martin Heidegger disputed the infallibility of truth in his *Parmenides* lecture course, where he defined the Greek *aletheia* not as "truth" as is typically done, but as "un-concealing," leaving intact the idea that revealing one thing necessarily conceals another. [2]

As we have shown, there exist multiple questions that science cannot answer. We tend to assume that science is the only source of access to true knowledge. Yet there exist in each specific natural or human science questions to which no certain answer can be provided. What is the origin of the universe? How did life appear on Earth? These issues are still being debated within the scientific community.

Given that science does not have a monopoly on answers to questions raised by humans and that some issues cannot receive a scientific response, the ideal that made science the model of all true knowledge finds its limits. Science does not provide, as often alleged, the only mode of response to the questions that humans raise.

Unlike philosophy that raises normative questions about what is just or what ought to be done, sciences are descriptive or positive. As such, the presumed superiority of the latter would significantly challenge the tenets of liberal arts education: "Suffice it to say that if Darwin's evolutionary account [. . .] is right, there is no scope for a universe with meaning, purpose, and intelligibility." [3]

Let us start with undermining the notion that scientific thinking is the only way to achieve true knowledge or that it was possible to answer scientifically the metaphysical questions concerning matters inaccessible to human experience.

In *Science: A Four Thousand Year History*, Patricia Fara claimed that "there can be no cast-iron guarantee that the cutting-edge science of today will not represent the discredited alchemy of tomorrow," [4] alleging that current science could be discredited in the future and that no scientists' research today could be totally immune from the test of time.

Aiming at developing a theory of everything, the cosmologist Stephen Hawking contended in *A Brief History of Time* that "we may now be near the end of the search for the ultimate laws of nature," [5] and twenty years later recognized in *The Grand Design* that scientists painted a picture of the universe that was different "from the picture we might have painted just a decade or two ago,"[6] thus acknowledging scientific fallibility and changing reality.

Understandably, scientific positivism was conceived on the idea that science could only provide answers concerning objects of experience and facts. Auguste Comte recognized that it should only explain how natural and human phenomena occur and never seek to give an answer to the question of why they occur, a metaphysical concern.

In light of the National Science Foundation (NSF) funding that went from being five times the size of their National Endowment for the Humanities (NEH) in 1979 to thirty-three times in 1997, the time has come to reverse the trend and to support liberal arts research that questions the meaning and finality of scientific inquiry.

If it is not possible to establish factual knowledge about the following critical inquiries (is the human soul immortal; is there a God; are human beings free?), it is nevertheless of the utmost importance to ponder them outside the scientific realm. In a world now at the mercy of nuclear conflagration, it is furthermore crucial to rethink how the humanities can bring to science what it is desperately lacking—meaning and purpose, for the hope and betterment of all humanity.

Giving a lecture at Cambridge University titled *The Two Cultures and the Scientific Revolution*, Charles Percy Snow discussed the importance of bridging the scientific and literary cultures of the time, which seemed to be distant and ignorant of one another. The scientists, he claimed, were incapable of reading and grasping the significance of an author like Dickens, while the specialists of the humanities ignored everything that was to be known about science.

In the book that followed his celebrated allocution, Snow was equally critical about the researchers who never read a work of literature and the liberal arts' scholars whom he associated with the British public at large, who were both "scientifically illiterate" and lacking interest on the subject. Refusing to come out in favor of either party, he dismissed by the same token the ignorant experts entrenched in their own specialization:

> A good many times I have been present at gatherings of people who, by the standards of the traditional culture, are thought highly educated and who have with considerable gusto been expressing their incredulity at the illiteracy of scientists. Once or twice I have been provoked and have asked the company how many of them could describe the Second Law of Thermodynamics. The response was cold: it was also negative. Yet I was asking something which is about the scientific equivalent of: Have you read a work of Shakespeare's?[7]

Those who hold that all questions can be answered by science should take Snow as a model and approach their study from interdisciplinary perspectives. In addition to earning a PhD in physics and conducting research on molecular structure, Snow also wrote novels about academic life. He sought to bridge both scientific and literary cultures.

By the early twentieth century, science fulfilled its promises of progress. From the infinite space of the universe to the molecular realm, from biological evolution to genetics, it had developed to such degree that it dramatically impacted people's daily lives. Witnessing the advancement of science and technology, humanists realized the extent to which the story of the world and the universe would need to be reconceived, along with their own thinking, beliefs, and analyses.

For their part, however, scientists seemed to celebrate their discoveries without fully measuring the new form of power it entailed. Both scientist and writer, Snow noted that a form of antipathy and incomprehension existed between the two camps that had a curiously distorted image of each other and found themselves impoverished by this disjunction.

The lack of dialogue to which he alluded between the two cultures did not do justice to the complex relationship that in fact existed between fields of knowledge. Researchers needed a system of thought through which they could consider the unity of the physical, biological, cultural, and social domains.

Reassociating the two cultures—one concerned with the laws of nature, and the other with questioning how to live—Snow found that the two paths (rationality and morality, the cognitive and the emotional, observation and action) were necessary for each other. While science transformed the knowledge and narration of the world, philosophy and literature represented and gave meaning to its conversions.

From the latter point of view, the universe becomes a poem that can be deciphered through a reconceived ethos. Leonardo da Vinci and Albert Einstein embody how the two cultures cohabit in the human mind. Their thought also illustrates the indeterminacy of scientific and artistic boundaries.

Informed by scientific knowledge, both are inspired by the realm of art. They perceive how, beyond pure logic, the imaginary enables them to explore further the correspondence between scientific and artistic queries and the interconnectedness of knowledge and being.

DA VINCI'S *HOSTINATO RIGORE*

From the humanities' point of view, integrating art into science can foster creativity: a scientist may become inspired and more imaginative through an artistic practice, for instance. Art can also help science shift paradigms by enabling its practitioners to see the world and the universe around us differently. The most outstanding thinkers in the scientific domain were also very creative people influenced by their interests in the arts.

If science offers empirical facts and develops theories, art's creativity transforms them into narratives that can have a moral, emotional, or spiritual significance. Leonardo da Vinci's drawing of the *Vitruvian Man* is illustrative of the unified relation between the humanities and sciences. Da Vinci was both artist and scientist, and he possessed an artistic and spiritual sense of the wonders that lay beyond the realm of science.

The human figure was, according to Vitruvius, the principal source and origin of proportion in classical architecture. At the intersection of art and science, the drawing illustrated da Vinci's understanding of proportion and of the analogy between the form and functioning of the human body and that of the universe.

This correspondence led da Vinci to rethink the art of the painter. The notes he took on the subject in *Le Trattato della pittura* attest to his reconsideration of technique and theory. Painting was for him the supreme achievement of spiritual activity. It was superior to sculpture that ignored the color and landscape, and to poetry because it explored in greater detail the "works of nature." Painting furthermore encompassed the totality of the real and the imaginary and as such constituted a permanent scientific inquiry. The progressive development of da Vinci's thinking entailed both artistic and scientific considerations.

The *Trattato* centered on the "philosophy of seeing": the capacity to grasp the workings of nature by acute observation. Every aspect of the book actually centered on the systematic understanding of the physical, mathematical, and geometric phenomena that determined visual perception. It was precisely through the application of logic, anatomy, and optics that painting was ennobled and could be put on the same plane as the other liberal and speculative arts such as philosophy, poetry, and theology.

Da Vinci was interested in all the branches of science. As a scholar, a single passion motivated him: the knowledge and understanding of the visible universe, in its structures and movements. His vision of the cosmos, founded on certain concepts in Platonism, revealed a series of harmonic forces enlightened with a great unity between the world of nature and the realm of the soul.

We need to underscore here the interdisciplinary rigor of his research. He never became a physicist like Copernicus or Newton, among those who revolutionized science through their discoveries or hypotheses. Yet his speculations led to a broader understanding of what constituted science or art and how the two were at some levels indivisible.

While celebrating the supreme certainty of mathematics, he was above all visual, one for whom the eye, "window to the soul," was the main path through which our intellect could fully appreciate the infinite work of nature. His universal curiosity rejected distinctions between pure and applied science, between fine arts and the mechanical arts.

Artist, scientist, engineer, architect, planner, botanist, and philosopher, Leonardo da Vinci exemplified the universal mind. His unpublished manuscripts reveal that the scientist was in him the equal of the artist and that his originality stemmed from his faculty to analyze, create, and synthesize.

One could contend that these capacities present in one individual offered C. P. Snow an invaluable support for his thesis. Known primarily as a painter but also engineer and inventor, da Vinci developed ideas far ahead of his time, such as the airplane, the helicopter, the submarine, and even the automobile. Few of his projects were realized or even feasible during his lifetime. Yet as a scientist, he did much to advance knowledge in the fields of anatomy, civil engineering, optics, and hydrodynamics.

The artistic dimension of his scientific research and experience was central in this respect, in the sense that it was conducive to his discoveries. Da Vinci observed and experimented with a rare gift of intuition and an infinite curiosity that equaled his power of invention.

Through comparison, rigor, and precision, reflected in his motto "hostinato rigore," da Vinci was able to approach scientific and artistic problems in broad terms. His reflection spanned a number of different subject areas and embraced all knowledge; he, the polymath, considered everything to be connected. He saw painting as the visual expression of a whole in which art, philosophy, and science were inseparable. By this token, those who did not have an appreciation for painting could love neither philosophy, science, nor nature.

In the words of Paul Valéry, what made da Vinci admirable was that, through this art and method, he challenged the traditional tenets of science, art, and philosophy. In his "Introduction to the Method of Leonardo da Vinci," Lawler explored through the artist the functioning of consciousness, the creative mind at work. To show the movements and successive moments of consciousness was not only to imagine the mental processes that marked each brush stroke of the great painter but also, and above all, to examine the work of a mind composing.

By basing and extending his reflection on observation, Valéry privileged the artist over the scientist. Thus, in the work of the painter, the act of seeing was rehabilitated as a sensory event because in reenacting the visible on the canvas, the painter experienced the visible by going back to the conditions and foundations of sight: "Most people see with their intellects much more often than with their eyes."[8]

Furthermore, contrary to science, the purpose of art is, among other things, to "unlearn" or "de-semanticize" the world. Since the work of art was meant to be seen again and again, not read or decoded in an instant, there would always be something more to see: "A work of art should always teach us that we had not seen what we see."[9]

Questioning the foundations of philosophical and scientific investigations, Valéry showed how the mind or thinking process derived more from sensory activities than the intellect. The visual and intellectual realms were assimilated to the functioning of the mind that, like the senses, remained linked to perceptual experience. Da Vinci was, from this point of view, one of the few artists who explored the Self, through science and art, or art alone when science did not suffice.

As art and science overlapped, it was difficult or impossible to maintain a clear distinction between sensation and thought, for no one knew where one ended and the other began. Da Vinci was a philosopher in this respect to the extent that his painting was, according to Valéry, a philosophy. The painter's reflection was born through the artistic creative process, and his pictorial activity could be regarded as a philosophy.

Postulating an allegory of human consciousness in his interpretation of Leonardo da Vinci, Valéry speculated how science was also an art and that its limits lay in its artistic dimension. The poet's drawings in the *Cahiers* sought to erase in this respect the artwork's material and temporal finitude. What emerged from his analysis of the mind was the provisional character of the artwork, which, as fragment of the inner life's creative process, challenged the finite scopes of science.

Like writing and drawing, science resulted from a provisional process, an artificial system of rules determined by language and convention, and, to that extent, an aesthetics or interpretation, in the same way Valéry's *Cahiers* belonged to the genre of science.

DECIPHERING EINSTEIN'S INTERDISCIPLINARY MIND

Einstein's scientific discovery of general theory was due, in part, according to Valéry, to the "artistic flair" of the physicist whom he considered the only artist among all true scientists. Attending one of Einstein's lectures on general theory gave Valéry a sense of the unity of nature. The artistic dimension the poet recognized in the scientist arguably played a significant role in the latter's research and discoveries.

Calling into question the principles of classical science, Einstein's quantum physics challenged the dichotomies between the discontinuous and continuity, chance and causality, the interdependence of atoms and their discreteness, the virtual and the factual, and probability and certainty. It thus profoundly transformed human perception of the phenomena of everyday life and contributed to the emergence of major currents of modern and postmodern thought.

According to Einstein's theory, time was no longer understood as an independent continuum, whereas based on classical mechanics, it was previously conceived as an absolute. With the theory of relativity, time was deprived of its independence. This discovery transformed the field of physics, which sought to understand and explain the natural phenomena of the universe. Attempting a study of the world in all its forms, physics achieved representations that were experimentally verifiable.

Quantum physics introduced different interpretations of the universe that could be considered to be true only to a certain point. It marked a break with classical physics by teaching us that at the atomic level it was difficult or impossible to predict the trajectory of an atom or an electron that was thus governed by probability. As such, it could not be an exact science. This also meant that there existed endless possibilities of scientific experience and understanding (through the notion of parallel worlds) and revealed the power of consciousness over matter.

Suffice to say that Einstein challenged many scientists and transformed science as much into a philosophy or religion. In fact, the more the smallest particles of the atomic world were examined, the more matter became an illusion, a sort of energy, which would mean that matter did not exist and that everything was made of élan or dynamism and information.

It is well established that Einstein's relativity, which undermined the foundations of science, was followed by Bohr's notion of indeterminacy, Heisenberg's uncertainty, and Gödel's incompleteness on the subject. Most people know that Einstein initiated the most famous equation in the world ($E = mc^2$), but many often ignore that he attributed his scientific discovery to his appreciation of music, particularly Mozart's through which he saw a reflection of the inner beauty of the universe.

Einstein's artistic experience was thus intimately related to his sightings. When studying Mozart, he was extracting experience and knowledge from an artistic and creative history. He was associating musical perception with the intuition that would be the driving force behind his scientific discovery.

It was at the age of thirteen that he first felt passionate for music. He suddenly saw in Mozart someone drawing from the invisible harmony of the world and giving it a musical expression. It was at about the same time in his life that he began to observe the nature of the speed of light, which would later constitute the subject leading him to the theory of relativity.

It is revealing that Einstein's insight into Mozart's music—music that drew upon the harmony underlying the world—occurred while he was questioning the nature of light, time, and space. His scientific inquiries that he named *Gedankenexperiment* used conceptual rather than actual experiments conducted in a laboratory. While he did not have the ability to physically test the idea of the simultaneity of time, he did it with "thought experiment."

In this regard, music nourished and shaped his mental landscape, giving it the imaginative force to glimpse the invisible principles at work within the scientific process. Imagination and music were for him important ways of knowing that were not limited to all that is known and understood at a given time; they embraced the entire world, and all there ever will be to know and understand: "I am enough of an artist to draw freely from my imagination. Imagination is more important than knowledge. Knowledge is limited; imagination encircles the world."[10]

Imagination, which for the poet Baudelaire was the "Queen of faculty," constituted a natural path toward innovation. Without it, the scientist could not question his assumptions to discover new phenomena. It spurred creativity, inquiry, and interdisciplinary thinking. It kept Einstein open to possibilities that would not have been conceivable had they remained tethered to the "purely" scientific domain alone: "One can have the clearest and most complete knowledge of what is, and yet not be able to deduct from that what should be the goal of our human aspirations [. . .]. Here we face, therefore, the limits of the purely rational conception of our existence."[11]

Granting primacy to imagination rather than the senses, reason, data, or knowledge, Einstein put in question the paths taken by scientists to reach the truth. He also challenged both the ultimate aims of science and the presumed superiority of scientific and mathematical facts to conceive of the laws of the universe. Stating that imagination was more important than knowledge implied that Einstein believed in the power of intuition and inspiration. Imagination was for him a true sign of intelligence that gave the capacity to understand the world. It ought to represent an essential feature of scientific research.

Einstein's observations challenge in their own way the emphasis that is currently put on science and math in today's education by underscoring how intuition and creativity are fundamental not only to the humanities but also to all academic inquiries. Whether in scientific, artistic, or literary studies, he deemed essential to recognize the limits of objective and quantitative knowledge and the importance of independent thought, and through it, the humanities:

It is not enough to teach man a specialty. Through it, he may become a kind of useful machine but not a harmoniously developed personality. It is essential that the student acquire an understanding of and a lively feeling for values. He must acquire a vivid sense of the beautiful and the morally good. [. . .] He must learn to understand the motives of human beings, their illusions, and their sufferings in order to acquire a proper relationship to individual fellow-men and to the community. [. . .] It is this that primarily constitutes and preserves culture. This is what I have in mind when I recommend the "humanities" as important, not just dry specialized knowledge.[12]

Contrary to scientists and/or academics for whom everything is purely logical and proceeds linearly from one point to another, Einstein argued that no great discoveries could be made when one proceeded logically based solely on what one already knew. They required what he called an intuition, a mind to be free to make cognitive leaps and uncover connections.

This means that prioritizing one discipline over another is harmful to innovation and research. A broad education is a necessary foundation to success in any field, and, by extension, that breadth should not cease early in the educational process but continue in some form through higher education and beyond. Composers such as Mozart could for example inspire the mind by introducing a singular melody or harmony that would lead the listener toward a higher plane of consciousness.

Music and physics revealed a beauty that was paramount to Einstein's conception of the universe. Inspired by the compositional structure and the inner unity he found in the music of Bach and Mozart, his work aimed at understanding the universe through a unified theory. Without the practice of music, he may never have made the discoveries that changed the world.

Beyond his scientific achievements, Einstein also represents a model to all students in arts and science for the active role he played in the City, and the extent to which he linked his academic research to what it could mean for people and the world. As scientist and musician, he was an active participant of society committed to causes that went beyond the scope of his studies.

He notably expressed his views on humanitarian, social, and societal issues on many occasions through articles and letters: "Each of us is here for a brief sojourn; for what purpose he knows not, though he sometimes thinks he senses it. But without deeper reflection one knows from daily life that one exists for other people [. . .] for the many, unknown to us, to whose destinies we are bound by the ties of sympathy."[13]

The book revealed the extent to which the breadth of his thinking reached far beyond the realm of science, and the extent to which the latter was not in itself sufficient to forge a system of values and beliefs through which he would conduct his life: "A positive aspiration and effort for an ethical-moral configuration of our common life is of overriding importance. Here no science can save us [. . .]. Fulfillment on the moral and esthetic side is a goal which lies closer to the preoccupations of art than it does to those of science [. . .]. The frightful dilemma of the political world situation has much to do with this sin of omission on the part of our civilization. Without 'ethical culture' there is no salvation for humanity."[14]

It is finally revealing that his approach to existential questions was more intuitive than intellectual, and that the arguably most important scientist who ever lived incessantly inquired about the spiritual dimension of humankind:

The most beautiful experience we can have is the mysterious. It is the fundamental emotion which stands at the cradle of true art and true science. [. . .] I
am satisfied with the mystery of the eternity of life and with the awareness and
a glimpse of the marvelous structure of the existing world [. . .] The man who
regards his own life and that of his fellow creatures as meaningless is not
merely unhappy but hardly fit for life. [15]

One recognizes in these few quotations how the unscientific dimension of
life was at the center of his reflections: the significance of intuitive experience and knowledge, the search for an equilibrium between giving and receiving, the pursuit of beauty, goodness, and truth, the need to give meaning
to one's life, and the recognition of the marvel of creation.

Einstein apprehended the mystical facet of existence, associating the
foundations of science with the mystery of life. His religious perception,
which resulted from personal experience rather than dogma, consisted in
expressing amazement and marveling before the harmony of the laws of
nature that revealed an intelligence superior to that of all humans.

The very cores of art and science centered on questions that arose in
considering humankind's origins. Such contemplations provoked introspection on life's mysteries and one's place in the world, both from a scientific
and humanistic viewpoint. If, as a scientist, Einstein sought to study objec-
tively without preconceptions the natural world, the spiritual explorer in him
was no less driven to pursue a deeper meaning in all things. As a scientist and
artist, he explored with great open-mindedness the great mysteries of the
spiritual order.

According to the opinions he shared in his writings, Einstein was a re-
searcher in both senses of the term, both material and spiritual. He remained
attentive to the intuitive plane of his being in spite of his exceptional intellect, arguing that, beyond the artifice and deception of knowledge, imagination was a liberating force that encompassed the entire world: "The true
value of a human being is determined primarily by the measure and the sense
in which he has attained liberation from the self." [16]

Einstein challenged the notion that science was purely objective and
superior to other domains while the arts were solely associated with the
subjective realm. Studying the history of religion, myth, art, and philosophy,
he demonstrated how the two paths in fact converged toward the same aim:
the search for meaning and a unified explanation of the universe.

TOWARD A POETICS OF THE UNIVERSE

Historically, humankind achieved through the arts a comprehensive understanding of the cosmos. During the modern period, however, emerged the
existence of a purely rational explanation of the universe through science that

led to the existence of two parallel cultures. Scientific and poetic minds such as Einstein's sought a return to their unity.

Art and science provide two ways to approach reality. When compared, it is striking that while the scientists' modern discoveries undermine the validity of their previous research, the artists' and poets' interpretations do not challenge the legitimacy of works sometimes composed centuries earlier. According to Victor Hugo, science, contrary to the arts, is vulnerable to time: "Science is continually changing in the benefit she confers [. . .]. What was ground yesterday is put into the hopper again today. The colossal machine, Science, never rests. It is never satisfied; it is insatiable for improvement, of which the absolute knows nothing."[17]

Another distinction between art and science rests, however, on the modern illusion that the latter can enable human advancement in a world deprived of any artistic or philosophical ideal. Poetry reveals for Hugo the eternal nature of beauty and truth and that all humans bear within themselves the eternal presence of music. Science by contrast was, according to Keats, powerful enough to clip an angel's wings, to dissolve beauty by conquering all mysteries. It was, for Edgar Allan Poe, a vulture that wilted wonder.

The poets reminded us also that their art was the first means by which humanity explored such questions as to what the world was made of, and how it came to be. In the sixth and fifth centuries BC, the pre-Socratics examined in verse these queries through their writing on physics, chemistry, and astronomy. Science was thus born in poetry. Lucretius's epic on atoms in *On the Nature of Things* pursued the long-established poetic tradition, renewed through the Romantic period, of exploring the temple of Nature and the secret of the universe.

Both poetry and science depended on metaphor, and if scientific subjects such as astrophysics or quantum mechanics relied on quantitative facts, they also concerned realities that went beyond human physical experience. In this respect, the truths of quantitative reasoning and scientific knowledge were not absolute; they were contingent and depended on analogy and representation. Einstein reminded his contemporaries that reality hinged on a human-made science that was limited to its means of illustrations and expression.

From this perspective, art, literature, and poetry could challenge mathematicians or scientists who equated their findings with truth and claimed that their theses and theorems could be reasonably considered factual independently of the universe. Pythagoras believed that the principles of mathematics were the foundation of all things, but his approach was also philosophical as he professed to be overall a lover of wisdom.

Galileo affirmed that mathematics was the alphabet in which God had written the book of nature. However, philosophy and poetry was also conceived from a vast book (that of the universe), according to Romantics and Symbolists, which incessantly opens our eyes to space, beauty, and awe. One could not comprehend the cosmos without knowing the mathematical but also poetic, philosophical, and mystical language in which it was written.

In *A Defense of Poetry*, Percy Shelley discussed the contributions poets had made to civilization over time. He contended that poetry in the broadest sense could teach us how to use scientific knowledge with wisdom and make us think about its bounds and inadequacies.

Poet Percy Bysshe Shelley pointed out the dangers that represented science's overabundance of facts with no way to process or make meaning of them, a problem he could uncover already in the Victorian period, and one that has only deepened. He wrote on the subject that "our calculations have outrun conception; we have eaten more than we can digest. The cultivation of those sciences which have enlarged the limits of the empire of man over the external world has, for want of the poetical faculty, proportionally circumscribed those of the internal world; and man, having enslaved the elements, remains himself a slave."[18]

More recently, Chet A. Bowers also focused on this line of thought in *Let Them Eat Data* in which he claimed that overreliance on computers and privileging of data collection over ethical meaning making has stunted our society's ability to deal with the problems of our time, such as economic inequality, environmental sustainability, and social justice.[19]

Contrary to what was alleged in scientific circles, Mary Midgley asserted that science could not answer all the questions relative to life. It could not fully explain what it meant to be human. Beyond the material world of atomic particles, the humanities (through literature, music, and poetry) revealed a facet of human existence unreachable through science.

A consideration for consciousness, intuition, awe, and sensation enabled a holistic interpretation of the role and place of humanity in the grand scheme of the universe. Midgley condemned in this respect the overemphasis on the sciences that was slowly occupying the spheres of thought in higher education and popular culture.

With so many thinkers across disciplines cautioning against our blind reverence of STEM over humanities fields and ways of knowing, it would be unwise not to make real changes in our values and approaches to education. We have thus far focused on the sciences but will now turn to how these questions play out with regard to technology.

JONAS'S ETHICS OF RESPONSIBILITY

In addition to his scientific discoveries, Einstein was also known for his civic engagement. Just as he defended the idea that science could provide a path to knowing the world, he also demanded that the search for truth be extended to social justice in the political realm. When FBI director J. Edgar Hoover ordered a wiretap of the scientist's phone communications and interception of his mail, it was under the pretext that he might have been a Russian spy.

Demonstrating his commitment to societal and global issues, Einstein chaired the Emergency Committee of Atomic Scientists, which aimed to raise funds to warn the public of the danger of nuclear weapons. In a letter through which he sought to collect donations, he wrote that scientists should feel a deep sense of responsibility regarding the extent to which they played a role in scientific developments that could be detrimental to life.

The committee raised $200,000 in order to inform Americans that new thinking and forms of higher consciousness were essential for humanity to survive the nuclear age. Einstein explained in his campaign that if we did not change our mentality and failed to develop a greater sense of human responsibility, we would die in an atomic confrontation.

Toward the end of his life, he used his celebrity to campaign for contentious political causes. One concerned the harassment and lynching of African American fighters returning from the war with the consent or participation of local police. He found it unacceptable that minority groups—returning to the southern United States from fighting fascism and nazism in Europe—would receive such treatment. Einstein called the White House, wrote letters, and participated in committee meetings against lynching with Paul Robeson and W. E. B. Du Bois. His battle against the evil of racism in the United States was one of his ultimate struggles for justice and equal rights.

We would contend here that Einstein represents a model to follow for STEM students not only for his scientific achievements but also for the degree to which he tied his research and findings to the outcome and effect they would have on people. Having escaped certain death in World War II when he fled Europe, and being involved indirectly in the development of nuclear weapons, Einstein felt that scientists had a role to play for the well-being of society and a responsibility to leave the world a better place for future generations.

This entailed a greater awareness of the plight of others around the world, a profound knowledge of history, and an appreciation of the cultural and artistic heritage of each world civilization, all of which came under the realm of liberal education and the humanities. He thus foresaw the immense danger that scientific and technological progress represented for the preservation of humanity's treasures and the very survival of the planet.

Einstein anticipated in that regard the work of Hans Jonas, who raised ethical questions that continue to be relevant to our times. To what extent can scientists and researchers control the means and ends, or uses and misuses, of technology? From a "value-neutral" perspective, human beings possess the capacity to determine the end and purpose of technology. Conversely, this ability is challenged from a "value-laden" viewpoint that supports the notion that technological progress is achieved independently of any human goal-oriented processes.

Percy Shelley's perspectives on the dangers of rapid technological advancement are in evidence as well in his wife, Mary Shelley's work; with her 1818 novel *Frankenstein*, she taps into a particular nineteenth-century misgiving about science and technology: their ability to create something that ultimately grows beyond human control. Significantly, Dr. Frankenstein's monster "becomes the oppressive master of man, although it was neither evil to begin with nor created out of deliberate malice."[20]

The Frankenstein myth demonstrates that any scientific or technological endeavor can prove to be humankind's undoing, despite the intentions of its creator(s), and the novel emphasizes that Dr. Frankenstein's tunnel vision—his never stopping to ask whether he *should* complete his work—is precisely the problem, and it is one we continually face.

In *The Technological Society*, Jacques Ellul shared the view that technological progress is independent of the human will, and he contested the scientists' and engineers' presumed power to steer, influence, and henceforth assume responsibility for the development of new technologies.

Hans Jonas, on the other hand, argued that it was imperative for scientists, mathematicians, and engineers to recognize and take personal responsibility regarding the choices they make and their implications for either the survival or destruction of humanity.

On this complex issue that involves the human will and capacity to forge its destiny and therefore the future of liberal arts education, philosopher Langdon Winner recently agreed that technological determinism is an unsatisfying perspective in that it does "little justice to the genuine choices that arise, in both principle and practice, in the course of technical and social transformation."[21]

If modern technologies offered humankind new possibilities, it was not in themselves that they could find their limits but in moral and ethical choices that for Jonas constituted the very essence of human experience. The author of *The Imperative of Responsibility* investigated the best way to live collectively, and he assessed the rightness and wrongness of human actions toward that end. Thus, from a teleological outlook, a morally right action was called to produce a positive outcome for all.

Ethics is not a science; it was founded upon human experience and narrative imagination. From this standpoint, the source of Jonas's ethics of responsibility was situated in the field of the humanities: literature, philosophy, and/or theology.

The question of individual and collective responsibility is raised, for example, by the Russian author Fyodor Dostoyevsky in *The Brothers Karamazov* in which the author claims through the voice of one of his characters his and all humanity's guilt. Philosopher and Talmudic commentator Emmanuel

Levinas likewise contended that if humankind downplayed its liability vis-à-vis others, it would deny its very essence, which was founded through its sense of responsibility. [22]

In *The Imperative of Responsibility*, Jonas began his reflection with the following question: Why should humanity exist? This existence that was taken for granted for many was no longer assured in his view. With the power of modern technology, humankind came to possess the capacity to destroy itself in little time. This fact required a reflection that had profound ethical implications. Pondering the problem at hand, Jonas found imperative that humankind should exist since it had, like any living creature, an inherent value that should therefore be protected.

In practice, this meant that any use of technology that threatened to destroy humanity should be prohibited. Jonas referred to this imperative by the formula *In dubio pro malo*. It meant that if several possible consequences of the utilization of technology existed, individuals and society should prepare for the most pessimistic outcomes.

Taking into account a new reality that could potentially affect the survival of the entire human race, we needed to rethink, according to Jonas, the premises of ancient ethics that were historically conceived through local interpersonal relations. The globalized technical-scientific preeminence of our modern societies now dominated and transformed the world (or nature) without knowing where it led. Ethics ought therefore to lessen its focus on the present and project itself into the future.

Jonas was often accused of being hostile to technology and its development. He, however, denied this accusation and even saw a need for the advancement of technology in order to remedy the damage it already caused so that it may not further harm the ontological durability of humankind.

STEM students must explore the ramifications of this imperative for their field and through this search rethink contentious issues that are today at the center of public debate: the foundation and justification of ethics, its relation to scientific and technological progress, humanity's mastery (or lack thereof) over life, the vulnerability of the environment, and the fragility of human life.

Modern technological power created new kinds of ethical problems unknown to date that fundamentally altered the essence of human action. Before the twentieth century and the aftermath of World War II, humankind could believe, rightly or wrongly, that the influence of technology on nature was limited. It was assumed that nature would restore its fundamental balance, and that for each new generation of living species, nature was exactly as the previous cohort had found it.

It was now a widely known fact, or should be, that the use of technology could have irreversible effects on nature. Its magnitude could be measured, for example, in the radioactive nuclear wastes that, though confined in disposal facilities, would remain harmful for thousands of years. Jonas contended, on that subject, that technological power imposed on humankind stipulations not only conducive to its development but also its maintenance.

One of the consequences of this endless growth of technical power was the need to repair damage caused by advances of technology with new technical innovations that themselves created new problems. [23]

Thus, modern technology behaved like a "nature," that is to say a necessity, an imposed framework; somehow, technology itself had spiraled out of control and needed to be tamed. This led Jonas to distinguish three powers: first, the one of humankind over nature acquired through technology without actually controlling it; second, the "self-sustained movement" of technology, real natural force without intelligence and without aim, which revealed the powerlessness of humankind to alter the course of its development; and third, the hypothetical power of humankind to control and master the development of technology.

The latter suppositions left open the possibility of human sway in the development of technology. Yet it seemed paradoxical or required a leap of faith. Could humankind control and save nature through the means of a technology over which it had no mastery? This indispensable domestication of an uncontrolled technology required anticipatory ethical reflections and actions. Jonas doubted that the developed countries might take restrictive measures conducive to it; he contended that if we did not, however, sooner or later nature would violently take us back to reality.

Today's news about global warming and the degradation of the environment attest to the validity of his argument. Jonas's concept of responsibility emerged from foreseeable catastrophe. It did not concern an experimental evaluation of what had been done but the determination of what needed to be done, how citizens should feel responsible about their behavior and its consequences, and the things that claimed their action. The real purpose of this new responsibility was the perpetuation of human life and its environment.

From the moment humankind had the power to destroy itself (or the living conditions for a future humanity), it also had new obligations. Jonas thought about the consequences of the atomic holocaust but also the presumed peaceful effect of the daily use of technology. If the danger of nuclear arsenals could be lessened or eliminated through conventions today, it would alter the well-being, interest, and fate of future generations.

A crucial lesson science and technology students must learn from Jonas is the notion that we are more than ever responsible for the world we leave beyond ourselves. This commitment comes in effect from a future that does not exist and yet must inhabit our conscience: "No previous ethics had to consider the overall condition and the future existence of human life." [24]

The ethics of responsibility thus rests on a nonreciprocal relationship since we are obligated unilaterally—by future humanity—to maintain the possibility of its existence. One must "act so that the effects of one's action are compatible with the permanence of an authentically human life on earth [. . .] and not destructive of the future possibility of life."[25]

Langdon Winner, in this respect, urges us to become more cognizant of the ways in which our technologies shape our lives: "As we 'make things work,' what kind of *world* are we making? [. . .] Are we going to design and build circumstances that enlarge possibilities for growth in human freedom, sociability, intelligence, creativity, and self-government? Or are we headed in an altogether different direction?" He continues: "Through technological creation and many other ways as well, we make a world for each other to live in. [Therefore] we must admit our responsibility for what we are making."[26]

The uncertainty concerning the preservation and survival of humanity defines a new horizon of humanity's responsibility. It is a matter of knowing which of our actions today, through our lifestyles, consumption of energy, and "interventions" on nature can endanger life or cause its disappearance in the future.

Such recognition also underscores the danger of an education solely driven by marketization, technologization, and the logic of maximization; the fragility of both human knowledge and ignorance; and the need of moral obligation in this context whose complexity must be addressed at all levels of schooling and irrespective of students' fields of study.

The mere possibility that uncontrolled technology could endanger the future existence or essence of humankind was sufficient to prohibit it unconditionally. Jonas rejected the belief that it would always be able to solve the problems it caused. It was more likely that its progress would pose more predicaments to resolve and that its successes needed to be feared as much as its failures.

Oriented toward the future of humankind, the ethics of responsibility needed a metaphysics founded on the rehabilitation of a *telos*. Jonas denounced in this respect the modern prejudice caused by the separation of being and value, *sein* and *sollen*, which, he insisted, only led to dogmatic assumptions that the natural sciences told everything there was to be known about life.

Such ethics responded to a fundamental need for the good that sided with Plato's idea discussed in *The Republic* against the emanation of a will devoid of any authority. Human beings were responsible for others but also for the whole biosphere that was perishable and needed care, and this obligation entailed a pedagogic, social, and political importance.

Humans had a debt vis-à-vis nature and the earth against which, in Jonas's words, a "sin" had been committed. It is striking that the philosopher drew an analogy between the protection of the planet and of a newborn child whose fragility requires constant attention. This commitment to the newborn represented, in his view, the source and model of all responsibility.

In conclusion, Jonas provided another illustration that brings us full circle: that of the statesman. Polity as society and civil government were at the heart of the necessity of responsibility, and it was clear that Jonas's imperative concerned the private conduct of citizens as much as public policy.

In the post–World War II era, the powerful forces of technology were unmasked if not fully measured, and their extension went beyond the grasp of STEM researchers. The magnitude of their impact required a collective political and social response, which calls to this day for a reconceptualization of scientific and technological training that must include a greater emphasis of what the humanities teach us through ethical and historical considerations.

A LIBERAL ARTS' PEDAGOGY FOR TECHNOLOGY?

In *Politics of Nature*, Bruno Latour rejected the hegemonic forms of science and technology that separated human from nonhuman (fauna and flora) interests, politics from ecology, and jeopardized the foundation of democracy that rested on the education of an informed citizenry and the search for the common good. Political ecology had "not yet begun to exist" in this view because decision makers still assumed that nature should be conquered and controlled,[27] a process that necessarily involved exclusion in the age of multiculturalism and multinaturalism.

The implication that scientific and technological progress resulted from an ideology and politics that supported the techno-industrial project of dominating the natural world led Latour to contend that the politicization of the sciences rendered ordinary political life impotent. We would argue that the mere juxtaposition of the words *ecology* and *politics*, which Latour underscores, calls for a renewed pedagogy of scientific and technological learning and research that takes into account its political facet.

Beyond academic fields' boundaries and objective facts, science and technology need to be studied in broad terms as Donna Haraway's concept of "situated science" suggests. Exploring the rhetoric and language of science through the mediation of technology creates the need for interdisciplinary critical research that can remedy the limits and inadequacies of disciplinary knowledge.

In this context, a pedagogy for technology requires a critical reflection about what it means to be a subject and a human being, as well as what our relation is to nature and technology. How does the latter's development modify human behavior in its essence? How does it put humanity and its environment in peril? The distance between our ability to foretell and our power to act—thought and action—constitutes a moral dilemma.

Students of science and technology must raise their awareness of self and others and question assumptions. They must foster their critical-thinking ability and a sense of civic responsibility. In light of the suffering caused by technology in human history, they must also nurture a capacity to care for others: "Faced with our own inclinations to cause harm, we must be both shocked and willing to face the reality."[28]

STEM students should also be taught that technology is not sufficient for human development. People's consciences and participation in the democratic process are much more crucial to fulfill the promise of the common good. Furthermore, as impressive as it may appear, its progress alone does not lead to ending poverty, improving the quality of life, and embracing the political and social aspirations of the disenfranchised.

Human advancement cannot solely be achieved through impersonal forces such as the market or high-tech evolution. Many in our society like to think so, according to Neil Postman, who asserts that it is "as if the question of what makes us better is too heavy, too complex—even too absurd—for us to address. We have solved it by becoming reductionists; we will leave the matter to our machinery."[29] Feeling impotent to create our own progress, Postman argues, we delegate that task to our technology.

There is no doubt that science and technology are powerful agents of transformation. It is, however, via the humanities that students can gain access to the full possession and expression of their faculties through language, ethics, and independent thinking. They open a path toward the future in that regard. Beyond technology's progress, human development entails the affirmation and rehabilitation of its dignity through the search for political, social, and environmental justice.

In this respect, Martin Luther King shared the notion that "moral progress" could easily fall behind the advancement of science and technology. In reference to those who are opposed to forces of social changes and progress, he pointed out that humankind suffered a "poverty of the spirit" that stood in contrast with a scientific and technological abundance.

> When the less sensitive supporters of the status quo try to argue against some of these condemnations and challenges, they usually cite the technological marvels our society has achieved. However, that only reveals their poverty of spirit. Mammoth productive facilities with computer minds, cities that engulf the landscape [. . .] these are awesome, but they cannot be spiritually inspiring. Nothing in our glittering technology can raise man to new heights, because material growth has been made an end in itself. [. . .] Another distortion in the technological revolution is that, instead of strengthening democracy at home, it has helped to eviscerate it. Gargantuan industry and government, woven into an intricate computerized mechanism, leave the person outside. The sense of participation is lost, the feeling that ordinary individuals influence important decisions vanishes, and man becomes separated and diminished. [. . .] Against the exaltation of technology, there has always been a force struggling to respect higher values.[30]

Martin Luther King underscored the spiritual and political dimensions of technology's influence. An inquiry about its use for the future thus required first and foremost a reflection about how to best serve the common good. STEM students must learn that, as useful as it might be, technology cannot fulfill by itself the need and aspirations for peace, justice, and solidarity, however prestigious its place in society might be. It ought not to promote a triumphant ideology ignorant of the plight of others, but should rather be the model for all humankind to follow.

The privileged position of technology prevents us more than ever from seeing its limitations and dangers. After the explosion of the first nuclear bombs on civilian populations in Hiroshima and Nagasaki on August 6 and 9, 1945, a fear regarding the power of science and technology was manifest, and brought about the following questions: Can we build the future of humanity only on scientific knowledge and technological advances? Are their values most appropriate to ensure the well-being of people and the planet as a whole?

The ramifications of scientific and technological developments on the social, economic, and political spheres are increasingly apparent and worrying. To promote a societal critical reflection on these issues presents a formidable challenge and demands a reconsideration of the objectives, approaches, and advances of science and technology that can easily lead to a form of cultural automatism and mechanization that reduce human introspective capability.

Current technological achievements do not have the same neutrality as ancient science. Critical analysis on the subject must enter the arena of public and educational debate. The teaching of technology through ethical perspectives is a matter of major importance, which also requires an overall reflection on the purpose of education itself, its *telos*.

We have seen how liberal arts education fosters the development of the individuals' and communities' critical and ethical conscience in that regard. Beyond the teaching of concepts, theories, and scientific processes, it promotes the emergence of an essential reflection about the paradigms and principles that constitute the foundations of technology in society. It also questions the power relation between knowledge, science, and society.

A liberal pedagogy of teaching technology also has existential and spiritual ramifications often lacking in scientific classrooms, as it would enable students to rethink historical events that involved the use and misuse of machinery driven by a material world devoid of transcendence.

It is worth noting that as Hans Jonas debated Heidegger's alleged affinities with Nazism during World War II, he began to sketch a philosophical argument against nihilism, which was in his view inherent to modern atheist existentialism and responsible for the lack of intellectual resistance to the inhumanity of Nazi ideology. Jonas aspired to a philosophy that could allow humankind to become part of a responsive world.

In a contribution concerning ethical problems in "Aktuelle Ethische Probleme aus jüdischer Sicht" ("Contemporary Problems in Ethics from a Jewish Perspective"), Jonas diagnosed the empty metaphysical void to which modern philosophical ethics had nothing to oppose. According to him, ethical relativism and indifference in the modern world had replaced the call for human responsibility.

It is in this context that he couched his reflections on the relation between technology and ethics, and on the limited mastery of humankind to restrain the irreversible effects that technologies could have on nature. In doing so, he emphasized the major difference between the present and past eras: the capacity of humankind to destroy itself.

Jonas also explained a few years before his death in 1993 that if we continued to make use of the earth as poorly as we did at the present time, the fate that threatened us became all the more certain. He warned against the menace of fatalism, almost as great as the danger of which humanity was now victim, and stressed the extent to which nature's ecosystems and humanity were endangered by technological advancements.

Exploring what a liberal arts' pedagogy for technology may require leads me to ask the following simple yet revealing question: Which science or technology major has read Jonas or questioned the implications of his/her study and research for the future of humanity? Jonas made clear that the divorce between humanity and nature would make it impossible to answer the techno-scientific challenges.

Investigating the question of responsibility through the philosophical and ethical angle of justification ("Should humanity exist?") was not for Jonas a matter of faith but of metaphysics. In this context, an affirmed existence entailed for him a concern for human life that transcended the dichotomies between human and nonhuman interests, politics, and ecology.

Paul Ricoeur summarized this perspective by writing that responsibility affirmed "the very possibility to say 'yes' to life, say 'yes' to the fact that we are already *in* life and into the world or even the very announcement of something as a vocation to which one has to remain faithful."[31] Human self-preservation was subject to a choice. Thus, life as such needed to be directed toward carefully defined ends, such as education, as being ought to affirm its existence against nonbeing.

In this respect again, Jonas underscored the limits of technology and the natural sciences in the understanding of life. Their disciplinary-centered methodological approaches did not permit considering nature as a whole. In fact, modern science was based on the elimination of final causes; Bacon and Galileo rejected the Aristotelian teleology.

Any notion of humanness could not be affirmed without a critical and philosophical inquiry. This implied for Jonas that science and technology ultimately needed to deal with being and altered forms of reality. Human experience could not be reduced to any deterministic or "materialistic" explanation.

From a liberal arts perspective, Jonas's pedagogy offered an essential perspective for STEM students because it contested the primacy of nihilism that refutes the ontological foundation of responsibility. It also challenged the subject/object dichotomy in two different ways: idealism was rejected because it separated humankind from real life, and materialism was defied because it only offered an incomplete vision of human life that could not be founded on values.

Reading Jonas's work, students learn therefore to question the opposition between *physis* and *techné*, nature and culture. They also find inspiration in his attempt to integrate humankind and nature in the field of ethical concerns. Refusing nihilism, he conceived of a responsibility through which humans would no longer treat nature as a mere object while striving to prevent its final anthropocentric consecration or sacralization.

THE CHALLENGES OF TRANSHUMANISM/POSTHUMANISM

Jonas's views have been challenged by the emergence of the transhumanist and posthumanist movements, according to which science and technology have permanently altered the course of human history that is now at a radical turning point. Extended to the nonhuman (cyborgs, clones, and robots), the human species seems to have lost its primacy in favor of previously unseen entities shaped by technology and that could mark its obsolescence.

More than a supplanting of the human, it could be contended that, from a liberal arts perspective, the transhumanist/posthumanist visions shed a new light on Jonas's thesis because they reveal at the same their potential benefits and dangers: on the one hand, the enhancement of human intellectual and physical capacities; on the other hand, the risk that technology could overcome entirely human limitations.

It is through the humanities—via moral, ethical, and overall critical approaches pertaining to cultural or feminist theories, to give examples—that STEM students must examine and explore the different facets of this choice and dilemma that concerns the future and survival of the human and animal species, and beyond, the entire biosphere.

Transhumanism represents a formidable challenge. It calls to improve through technology humanity's corporeal and mental capabilities but also alleviate significant aspects of the human condition relative to disability, suffering, sickness, aging, or death, recognizing them as unnecessary or undesirable. It makes the human anachronistic and passé, highlighting the provisionality of its being and existence.

At its best, transhumanism can seek to apply science and technology in order to win the battle against poverty, disease, malnutrition, and dictatorial governments in the world. It can be rooted in the humanism of the Renaissance and the Enlightenment. Pico della Mirandola called for humankind to "sculpt its own statue," and according to Darwin, it became probable that humanity as we know it may not be in the final stage of its evolution but rather at a beginning stage.

In 1957, biologist, eugenicist, and proponent of natural selection Julian Huxley contended that humans could better themselves through science and technology. He defined the transhuman as a human remaining human but simultaneously transcending itself by deploying new possibilities of and for its human nature. Transhumanism thus shares several values with humanism, among them a respect for reason and science, a commitment to progress, and a great consideration for human (or transhuman) existence in this life.

According to its advocates, people necessarily embrace the progress of technology since everyone wants to be smarter and escape from illness or death. Transhumanism affirms that it is possible and desirable to aim at improving human capabilities. From this perspective, it does not abandon the concept of free and autonomous individuals embraced by liberal education, and it extends the Enlightenment project of human emancipation through scientific progress.

This leap of faith, however, requires careful considerations that only the humanities provide: What innovation should be promoted and what amelioration sought? How would either embrace the tenets of ethics, social justice, and the common good? To what extent and for what purpose would they put an end to the presumed legitimacy of human dominion over the natural world, and transform the interrelations between human and nonhuman creatures?

If there exists a potential that the development and usage of technology will enable us to surpass the constraints inherent to human nature, the outcome following the emergence of artificial intelligence and techno-culture remains highly uncertain. Similarly, the consequences of the interactions between the embodied human subject and intelligent machines, opposing an ethical dynamic to a technological one, are unknown.

According to Katherine Hayles, "There are no essential differences or absolute demarcations between bodily existence and computer simulation."[32] The "posthuman" thus emerges as a deconstruction of the liberal humanist notion of what being "human" may represent.

One thing to consider here is that transhumanism differs from liberal humanism in that the former focuses specifically on the contributions of technology to human problems but seems to turn away from the concerns of social justice and the needed reform of human institutions. It abandons the aims of historical and traditional humanism to implement progressive polity.

Yet transhumanism is not politically neutral, according to Jacques Ellul, who saw its development as a direct corollary of capitalism and more generally of the productivist ideology. If transhumanism aligned itself to capitalism, it was first and foremost because it reinforced inequalities. Ellul considered that it was not technology itself that enslaved humans but the sacred dimension that they gave to it. As an autonomous phenomenon, it was escaping more and more from human control.

According to Martin Heidegger, humankind is unfree and chained to technology. It is altering our cognitive perception of reality, our relation to nature. As a mode of revealing (*aletheia*), the end of the technicalization of reason and knowledge was human instrumentality. Reality became technologically determined. The only way to exist for humans was to become a technological, energy-resource to be transformed and used, unless humanity was able to reorient itself.

Beyond socioeconomic concerns, both transhumanism and posthumanism posed political, pedagogical, and existential problems. Advocating the improvement of human genetic traits, eugenics policies are vulnerable to abuse, the criteria of natural selection being determined by individuals or government bodies that hold constitutional power. Nazi eugenics, for example, represented a fundamental and infamous encroachment upon human rights.

The gap between the technical achievements that scientists have made and the murderous path of their use calls for an "eschatological" reflection about the ultimate ends of human attainments. For humans who seek progress, there must be an ethical imperative to contemplate. Should we leave it to technology alone to remedy the ills of the world?

If the danger is real, we would contend like Jonas that technology is not a totally autonomous phenomenon and that we must attempt to define its aims and possibly have control over its achievements. If humankind partially leaves its future in the hands of technology, it must be with an intent that the latter will not assert its will to power. When it is manifest, the blind reliance on technology—or as Langdon Winner refers to it, "technological somnambulism," or sleepwalking[33]—is symptomatic of dehumanized societies that are prone to existential threats.

The film *Gattaca* exposes the struggle of an unmodified human being, Vincent Freeman, born with "natural" defects and qualities in a world where biotechnological improvement, genetic transformations, and discriminations have become the norm. Vincent's impediment is embodied in *The Terminator*'s trailer, a film in which a global artificial intelligence, Skynet, having reached consciousness, decides to exterminate humankind to avoid being disconnected by its creators.

In both instances, nanotechnologies promote exclusion and segregation. They also raise philosophical and ethical issues related to the scientific manipulation of human genes, enhancing humanness to a supposedly superior life and intelligence.

Taking into account that technological advances led to the creation of artificial intelligence whose capacities are called to exceed those of humans, can the liberal humanism of antiquity and the Renaissance remain a relevant philosophy, or should it be abandoned?

For those who believe that humanity is destined to disappear, posthumanity is portrayed in the guise of something other than or beyond human. They consider that through its ingenuity, humankind will soon not have the need to be born because it will be self-produced. It will no longer know disease because nanorobots will repair it permanently. It will not die except to voluntarily delete the downloaded content of its "consciousness."

STEM students taking courses in the humanities such as literature, culture, philosophy, or critical theory need then ask: How will "we" live in this world? What ethics will put us in harmony with a wider humanity, capable of including animals as robots or cyborgs and of merging an organic being and a machine? What rights should be afforded to these robots in charge of making our lives "more human"? The transhuman and posthuman utopias present formidable challenges. It is precisely through them that the greatness of being human and of the humanities may be revealed or annihilated.

NOTES

1. René Descartes, *Discourse on Method and Related Writings* (New York: Penguin Classics, 1999), 44.

2. Martin Heidegger, *Parmenides*, trans. André Schuwer and Richard Rojcewicz (Bloomington: Indiana University Press, 1998).

3. Alex Rosenberg, *Philosophy of Science* (London: Routledge, 2000), 10.

4. Patricia Fara, *Science: A Four Thousand Year History* (Oxford: Oxford University Press, 2010), 364.

5. Stephen Hawking, *A Brief History of Time* (New York: Bantam Books, 1988), 157.

6. Stephen Hawking, *The Grand Design* (New York: Bantam Books, 2010), 14.

7. Charles Percy Snow, *The Two Cultures and the Scientific Revolution* (Eastford, CT: Martino Fine Books, 2013), 15–16.

8. James R. Lawler, ed., "Introduction to the Method of Leonardo da Vinci," *Paul Valéry: An Anthology* (Princeton, NJ: Princeton University Press, 1977), 49.

9. Lawler, "Introduction to the Method of Leonardo da Vinci," 50.

10. George Sylvester Viereck, "What Life Means to Einstein." *Saturday Evening Post*, October 26, 1929.

11. Albert Einstein, *Ideas and Opinions* (New York: The Modern Library, 1994), 45.

12. Einstein, *Ideas and Opinions*, 72.

13. Einstein, *Ideas and Opinions*, 8–9.

14. Einstein, *Ideas and Opinions*, 56–57.

15. Einstein, *Ideas and Opinions*, 11–12.

16. Einstein, *Ideas and Opinions*, 12.

17. Victor Hugo, "The Art and Science," *William Shakespeare* (Freeport: Books for Libraries, 1970), 105.

18. Percy Bysshe Shelley, *Political Writings including A Defense of Poetry* (New York: Appleton-Century-Crofts, 1970), 190.

19. C. A. Bowers, *Let Them Eat Data* (Athens: University of Georgia Press, 2000).

20. Gerald Holton, ed., *Science and Culture: A Study of Cohesive and Disjunctive Forces* (Boston: Houghton Mifflin, 1965), 192.

21. Langdon Winner, "Technologies as Forms of Life," in *Readings in the Philosophy of Technology*, ed. David M. Kaplan (Lanham, MD: Rowman & Littlefield, 2004), 107.

22. Emmanuel Levinas, *Entre Nous: On Thinking of the Other* (New York: Columbia University Press, 1998), 133, 223.

23. Hans Jonas, *The Imperative of Responsibility: In Search of an Ethics for the Technological Age* (Chicago: The University of Chicago Press, 1985), 245.

24. Jonas, *The Imperative of Responsibility*, 26.

25. Jonas, *The Imperative of Responsibility*, 30–31.

26. Winner, "Technologies as Forms of Life," 112.

27. Bruno Latour, *Politics of Nature: How to Bring the Sciences into Democracy* (Cambridge: Harvard University Press, 2004), 2.

28. Nel Noddings, *Educating Moral People: A Caring Alternative to Character Education* (New York: Teachers College Press, 2002), 8.

29. Neil Postman, *Building a Bridge to the 18th Century* (New York: Vintage Books, 1999), 41.

30. Martin Luther King Jr., *A Testament of Hope: The Essential Writings and Speeches of Martin Luther King, Jr.* (New York: HarperCollins, 1991), 644.

31. Farhang Erfani, ed., *Paul Ricoeur: Honoring and Continuing the Work* (Lanham, MD: Lexington Books, 2011), 159.

32. Katherine Hayles, *How We Became Posthuman: Virtual Bodies in Cybernetics, Literature, and Informatics* (Chicago: University of Chicago Press, 1999), 3.

33. Winner, "Technologies as Forms of Life," 107.

Chapter Four

Transcendent Humanities

The humanities encompass a broad range of academic fields including literature, art, history, languages, and philosophy. They give access to the narrative imagination of different individuals and cultures around the world, and stimulate students' critical thinking, significantly widening their perspectives and awareness of the human condition. They enable them to escape the limits of the individual's presence.

Even more far-reaching, we have seen how they are essential to rethinking our understanding of the social and physical sciences. We examined in chapters 2 and 3 how literature and the arts provide insights that are indispensable for students engaged in the study of economics, science, and technology. They help students of all disciplines explore from a human-centered approach the relation between knowledge and power, and the importance of higher education for the development of democracy, ethics, and justice.

Similarly, poetry and theater expose students to tragedy but also teach how to surmount obstacles. They give meaning to human experience and explore the interrelation of self and others, society and the world. Philosophy conveys the wisdom needed to face up to the crisis of legitimacy brought forth in our postmodern civilizations. It enables us to broaden our knowledge and alertness, to formulate new ends and ideals—politically, socially, symbolically, and allegorically.

TRANSMITTING HERITAGE

The humanities comprise an ensemble of fundamentally valuable knowledge of an essentially different nature from that of the scientific and technical. The study of ancient and modern languages and literatures, history, art, philosophy, and religion are crucial to assessing the potential use and misuse of science and technology and to give purpose and meaning to their progress for the construction of a just and ethical world, as well as to the well-being and even survival of humanity.

How could one then explain the erosion of the value granted to the humanities and the indifference they generate? The first explanation is the emergence of the digital, a new religion called to abolish and replace the ancient forms of education of the mind and fostering of the imagination.

Technology may be useful; it cannot, however, supplant the humanities that have proven their importance in promoting students' independent judgment and thinking across boundaries. The "all digital" approach in education leads to the triumph of the sheeplike mind and the eventual disappearance of individuals endowed with a critical-thinking ability that the anonymous geeks' social networking would replace.

In addition, the short-sighted utilitarian approach to an "all economic" education can only conceive of schooling in terms of immediate returns. It zealously tramples the most precious jewels of our symbolic heritage: language, memory, beauty, taste, and the sensitivity of the mind and heart.

As a counterpoint to those who question the usefulness of the humanities, a purely utilitarian education would lead to an unchallenged quantitative assimilation of facts and data. Except in high-level professional training, what is useful to our technical and digital world is learned very early on in students' youth through their daily experience, more than in theory or criticism. It is not by relying on the spontaneous appropriation of the digital world that schools and universities will stimulate the minds of our future leaders. However, those who learn against the flow of uncritical common knowledge will be awarded an education worthy of respect.

The study of the humanities, including foreign languages, provides students' minds prospects of which the exclusive value of the immediate and useful deprive them. Messengers of a distant and different world, to many students the Swahili, Mandarin, Arabic, or Hindi languages open the mind to difference and to cultures other than one's own. Through them, students receive the required experience to step back from their own habits and perspectives, and to explore other worlds with a critical distance. Then, the preconditions for the exercise of a liberated mind begin to be fulfilled.

Montaigne's *Essays*, as an example, are based on a constant comparison between the tragic events of the late sixteenth century in Western Europe and the lessons of Greek and Latin authors who had also experienced conflicts and civil wars. The fields of literature, history, arts, and cultural anthropology counterbalance through their cognitive points of view all forms of colonial utilitarianism. They owe much in fact to the Greco-Latin humanities.

The travelers and missionaries of the eighteenth century would not have made the effort to understand and save the languages, mythologies, works of art, and cultural artifacts discovered by explorers if they had not been educated to study and preserve, in the footsteps of the sixteenth-century humanists, the languages, mythologies, arts, and manners of classical antiquity.

If students wish to be educated to respect other cultures, no better preparation than the one offered through the humanities can lead them to admire and understand the various civilizations threatened by our globalized world. If it is right to have expanded the theoretical, cultural, and geographic realms of the humanities in the twentieth and the twenty-first centuries, it is also essential to remember and learn where they originated in a Western perspective, so as to reveal the lens through which these different cultures are viewed.

Transcending the humanities from this standpoint entails the necessity of diffusing and transmitting their heritage to students and the public at large concerned about the current state of education. But to pass down from generation to generation the literary and artistic treasures of the past does not simply mean to hand over artifacts and factual information. It is to give future generations the tools to exercise their freedom of mind, thought, and spirit.

The humanities provide a fruitful dialogue with the best minds of even those of our distant past, of a long dialogue resulting from an astonishing diversity and novelty. It is this exciting transmission from professors to students that one needs to perpetually rediscover and internalize.

The loss of value conferred to the humanities instigates the decline of a different aspect of our relationship to the world. This undervalued mode, allegorical and not algorithmic, analogic more than logic, gives us access to the realm of quality, flavor, ambiguity, beauty, love, and taste, which determines our happiness and well-being. Being educated through the practice of the arts, letters, and poetry frees young souls who, as prisoners in a technical and utilitarian world, increasingly ignore themselves and others.

In a world dominated by social media, Sherry Turkle showed recently how the art of storytelling and the traditions of oral history and conversation, our most humanizing experiences, are being lost because they embody qualities antithetical to the technological imperatives of mass society, qualities such as time to develop a thought, self-reflection, and our capacity for empathy.[1]

What we have also lost, or rather forgotten and ignored in this other world, is the true home of our senses and minds, the imaginative way of knowing artistically and poetically. Less advanced than us in the abstract and the technical, past authors and readers had a more direct relation to and experience with the world and universe that they explored through metaphors.

> Nature is a temple in which living pillars
> Sometimes give voice to confused words;
> Humans pass there through forests of symbols

Which look at them with understanding eyes.
Like prolonged echoes mingling in the distance
In a deep and tenebrous unity,
Vast as the dark of night and as the light of day,
Perfumes, sounds, and colors correspond.

Based on a transcendental or metaphysical vision, the poem "Correspondences" that we translate here from memory alleges the predominance of nature over humankind, which is called to decipher its mystery. The poet's task is to provide an "Orphic explanation" of the Earth. Thus, Baudelaire considers the external world as a text, with this question: What is it endeavoring to say? From an anthropological perspective, the poet alludes to the mystery of human existence.

Literary and artistic masterpieces have left us with profound paths of listening, feeling, and knowing from which we are increasingly exiled through the use of technology. Our screens inhibit us from seeing the world of qualities and tastes and isolate us from our five senses, diminished and perhaps annihilated by the display of the digital tablet. Yet through the classical authors, the past (recent or more ancient) provides keys to reopen the doors of perception and comprehension. They transcend vertically, horizontally, and cross-culturally the notion of "the examined life" which, according to Seneca, liberates the mind from the bondage of custom and habit.

Contemporary academics such as Derek Bok and Andrew Delbanco, who have criticized the marketization of universities, perceive this need for transcendence in higher education when they contend that the humanities cannot remain distant from issues that concern the fate of humanity. The sole purpose of the university should not be to prepare students for the marketplace. Narrowing the scope of its raison d'être to utilitarian values imperils Seneca's vision that all citizens be trained in the arts, literature, philosophy, and critical thinking so that they can call their minds their own.

As we have established in the preceding chapters, the fundamental justification of liberal arts education is to offer students a broader view and understanding of human experience that other disciplines do not provide: the search for meaning and human purpose on earth, an appreciation for empathy and cross-cultural awareness, knowledge of self and others.

BIBLIOTHERAPY AND HEALING HUMANITIES

The value of the liberal arts should be assessed, beyond the lens of marketability, in societal, existential, and transcendental terms. Advocating the importance of the humanities and seeking to reestablish bridges between the university and society require students to overcome the limits and boundaries of disciplines in order to fulfill the promise of an education based on emancipationist humanism.

Bibliotherapy has demonstrated in this respect how literature possesses the power to liberate the mind from the bondage of obliviousness by raising consciousness about one's place in the world. Like art and music, it also heals the mind and soul by restoring the emotional and psychological health of patients affected by the disorders of the modern world. Millions of people including students suffer from depression and mental illness today, while millions of others live in jail, physically and psychologically, both perpetrators and victims of violence who embody the ills and sufferings of society.

A sentence attributed to Victor Hugo ("He who opens a school door, closes a prison") illustrates the liberating effect and therapeutic dimension of liberal arts education. The author of *Les Misérables* contended that books were lighting up the world, and that learning to read was like lighting a fire.

As a therapeutic means, reading literature eases mental health disorders (e.g., anxiety, depression, and phobias) and strengthens psychological well-being. Many studies have delivered convincing results about its effectiveness, so that today its practice in medicine is recognized. Among the most notable impetus in the scope of this field is a program launched by the Reading Agency that prescribes a library subscription with a list of suggested books for mental health disorders as a remedy.[2]

The history of bibliotherapy brings us back to the time of Plato and Epicurus, during which the practice of philosophy was associated with the assurance of good mental health because it stimulated the organization of thought and action through reason. The practice of philosophy was based on rational thought that the Greeks opposed to emotional submissiveness, which was the source, according to the Stoic school, of all the ills of the soul.

Reason thus countered the maladies named "desire" and passion because it enabled intellectual distance. It is on these therapeutic foundations that contemporary bibliotherapy was built, through a renewed perception and rationalization of the self and the world as a means of soothing a troubled patient. From an ancient Greek perspective, the library constituted a healing place for the soul.

Much later, in a text about the meaning and importance of reading, Marcel Proust explores the state of individuals experiencing what we would call moderate or major depression today, and how reading could bring about psychotherapeutic care. Proust observes that fragile minds could fall in a state of inertia, entangled in self-denial and unable to want or desire. To find again a taste for yearning, including that of healing, the author believes that these individuals should find help through the intercession of an external mind (a novel's narrator or character), and achieve, through a therapeutic reading, a solitary and salutary introspection.

Bibliotherapy emerged as Marcel Proust was writing his masterpiece *À la recherche du temps perdu* (*In Search of Lost Time*). In the middle of World War I, in 1916, doctors and librarians from military hospitals used books to alleviate the post-traumatic suffering of soldiers returning from battle. A set of readings was selected as an instrument of therapeutic medicine and psychiatry, and as means of relieving trauma and distress.

To this day, a classical repertoire comprised of novels, poetry, biographies, and fictional works enhance patients' wellness through an identification process ultimately leading to empathy. The organization Reading Agency pursues its program with the goal of finding the most suitable books for six million people suffering from psychological fragility in Britain. To begin with, a list of thirty items is established by professionals and health experts and prescribed after medical consultation. The School of Life based in London also proposes a therapeutic program, including "group bibliotherapy" where patients discuss their impressions of a recommended book and its effect on their psyche.

The effectiveness of bibliotherapy in Britain was corroborated in a recent study published in the scientific journal *PLOS ONE*. A team of researchers brought together over two hundred patients diagnosed with depression: 65 percent of participants had a history of mental disorders and 80 percent of these patients' disorders were classified as severe. Half received antidepressants, and the other followed a therapy program that required the reading of the work *Overcoming Depression* and related discussions with psychologists.

After four months, the results were salient: 42.6 percent of reader-patients experienced significantly reduced levels of depression against 24.5 percent of the medicated patients. After a year, the first group was better able to manage depression than the second. It was also found that of all the subjects, 59 percent said they had read a book that was psychologically beneficial.

A specific list of books was assigned to respond to the particular needs of patients. The conundrum of accepting oneself was alleviated through the reading of Saint-Exupéry's *The Little Prince* and Whitman's *Leaves of Grass*. Those who had difficulties coming to terms with aging read Joyce's *Dubliners* and García Márquez's *One Hundred Years of Solitude*.

The patients seeking meaning and beauty read Proust's *In Search of Lost Time*, and the ones experiencing exclusion were assigned Steinbeck's *Of Mice and Men* and Camus's *The Stranger*. The reading to overcome hardship was Isabel Allende's *The House of the Spirits* and Homer's *Odyssey*; to know oneself and others: Jon Krakauer's *Into the Wild* and Lore Segal's *Her First American*; to reconnect with the spiritual realm, Saint-Exupéry's *Wind, Sand and Stars*.[3]

Among the forms of benefits experienced by respondents, the most cited were that they could identify and understand their problem and realize that they were not alone, and that they felt "helped" and compelled to gauge the nature of their condition from a new point of view. The study highlighted a convergence between individual experiences and their readings' therapeutic virtues. Inspired by Greek philosophy, and praised by Marcel Proust in the early twentieth century, the appeasement of psychological sufferings and the strengthening of psychological well-being through literature was "scientifically" demonstrated.

Exploring self, meaning, and beauty in the face of the suffering and anxiety of life through historical narratives, literary fiction, memoir, poetry, and storytelling provide a unique understanding of the human condition in all its complexity. Literature establishes a means of memory and action and a path toward identification, catharsis, insight (meaning), healing, and empathy (emotional response).

As psychologists David Comer Kidd and Emanuele Castano at the New School for Social Research in New York have argued, reading fiction represents a valuable socializing influence.[4] The specific study's suggestions were that students be exposed to the examination and understanding of literary genres, memoir, historical and creative fiction, poetry and storytelling, and acquire interpretive skills. Reading provided a path to healing by altering one's sense of individuality, and enhancing one's capacity to empathize.

REMEMBERING AUSCHWITZ

Trauma study has shown how identification and empathy for the other make each individual partake in the process of collective memory. Through a transference of affect, it leads students to ponder the need for ethical and political action to remedy past and present injustices. Transcending ethnic and national boundaries, readers and authors attest to the past. They identify with the victims and acquire an ethics of remembrance.

Giving a witness account of the annihilation of the Jews by the Nazis in concentration and extermination camps, Holocaust literature partakes in this process. Detained in one of the ghettos where the Jews of Europe were held in captivity, the Polish-Jewish historian Emanuel Ringelblum documented the daily life in Nazi-occupied Warsaw by collecting texts and diaries from the members of his community.

After the war, the Holocaust became a prominent literary and philosophical subject. Survivors faced, however, the challenge of writing about an unprecedented event marked by horrific experiences. How could they find the words to describe or convey their true nature? Art and literature could be the only path through which they could both attest to what happened and keep alive the memory of the fallen. Through diverse literary genres, from testimonies to philosophical essays and poetry, they make palpable the horrors of the Holocaust and the suffering and despair of its victims and survivors.

In Primo Levi, who narrates his daily struggle to survive at Auschwitz, the reader grasps the victims' sufferings and perceives "the traumatic experiences of others as experiences one might oneself have had, and of inscribing them into one's own life story."[5]

In the aftermath of the war, thousands of testimonials, novels, poems, and essays were published on the subject. The Holocaust was a negation of humanity in its societal, moral, and existential foundations. It led surviving witnesses to examine what constituted being human and the nature of humanness, and to devote several books on analyzing the experience of the extreme, the effects of terror and humiliation, and the psychological and moral impacts of outright deprivation.

Primo Levi's *Se Questo è un uomo* and Robert Antelme's *L'Espèce humaine* recounted their knowledge of the camps with the sole purpose of restoring to humankind its dignity. In their exhausting battles against Nazi barbarism, their main weapon was language and literature. Robert Antelme contended in this respect that unlike the animal species, humanity was not defined by race. A human species existed, and the Nazi crime against humanity was to have attempted to establish categories of humans, such as the Aryan race, as if there were inferior or superior categories.

Questions pertaining to human nature and the relation between the human and the inhuman have continued to consume philosophers and intellectuals after Auschwitz. The different approaches and genres of writing include historical documents, biographical narratives, and critical reflections. The meanings that they ascribe to such an event are no less broad and diverse. Raising fundamental questions about the functions and limits of literature, the writing of history, and ultimately, the humanities, these witness accounts enable students to explore the diversity of human experience, what it means to be human, and the power and responsibility that it entails.

Hannah Arendt rid the interpretation of the camps' extermination of any mystical or religious dimension in her famous thesis on the banality of evil. She saw the Nazis as servants of crime, in a huge administrative machine that had gone mad and inhuman. Reporting on the trial of Adolf Eichmann for *The New Yorker*, she noted that the Nazi mass murderer had not expressed a sense of remorse or moral responsibility for his activities, motivated by professional promotion as much as by ideology. Her analysis thus challenged the objective relevance of morality and ethics in human actions.

Focusing on the relation between remembering and forgetting, and the link between the perception of historical experience and the writing of historical narrative, Paul Ricoeur considered for his part how the constructive process of remembering could come at the expense of others in a given period of history. From this angle, Ricoeur underscored the challenge of representing the past. Since memory operated in the wake of the imagination, any historian should be critically aware of the link between the latter and the former.[6]

By questioning the suitability of writing poetry after Auschwitz, Adorno raised other issues concerning the limits of literature and the aporetic writing of history that would later be examined in Maurice Blanchot's *Writing and Disaster* and Jacques Derrida's *Writing and Difference*. Adorno asserted that writing poetry after Auschwitz was barbaric. The survivor who wanted to bear witness to the event was faced with the limit of transcribing the nature of the experience to the extent that the Holocaust, the reality of the concentration camps, and the suffering it engendered seem to go beyond the scope of literature and human comprehension.

Adorno's contention went a step further when he argued that criticism found itself faced with the final stage of the dialectic between culture and barbarism. Writing literature, the belief in intellectual progress, and critical intelligence could not subsist after the Holocaust.

Adorno's perplexing verdict refuted the poet Paul Celan, who affirmed that art needed to fill the void and impasse left by the Holocaust. For Adorno, the radical gap between the signifier and the signified caused by the indescribable nature of the Shoah could not be alleviated through writing. Poetry could not respond to what was ungraspable. If it spoke, it would be meaningless. Even though the poets and artists could not be silenced, writing poetry could no longer achieve its ostensible aims.

Recalling his experience with his father in the Auschwitz concentration camp, Elie Wiesel associated these years with the death of God and his disgust with humanity. All seemed to come to an end, from religion and literature to humankind: "Never shall I forget that nocturnal silence that deprived me, for all eternity, of the desire to live. Never shall I forget those moments that murdered my God and my soul and turned my dreams to ashes. Never shall I forget those things, even were I condemned to live as long as God Himself. Never."[7]

Reading these lines, students experience a moment of epiphany asking themselves how could such a thing happen, how could it be avoided in the future, and what is their responsibility before others? Auschwitz seemed to deny the legitimacy of human life. The brutality of the extermination camps suppressed not only the possibility of the present and future but also of the past. The ancient codes, once immediately decipherable by the Ashkenazi community, were suddenly deemed inappropriate and irreplaceable.

Adorno's claim that poetry would be impossible was countered by Primo Levi and followed by the publications of many survivors' texts. Not only did the poets surviving the camps and ghettos continue to write, but their work allowed the Yiddish language to find a rebirth. Authors drew their inspirations from the metaphors, rhythms, breaths, and symbolic forms of the Jewish literary tradition that had structured their imagination.

The poet Jacob Glatstein, author of *The Joy of the Yiddish Word*, and the theologian Abraham Joshua Heschel partook in the spiritual rebirth of Jewish culture as Jews struggled to preserve their spiritual heritage in the post-Holocaust era, yet still witness of the destruction of the European Jewry that would continue beyond 1945 in the Soviet Union. The Russian Yiddish poets Peretz Markish, Leyb Kvitko, and Itzik Feffer, who lived a few years after the defeat of nazism, were murdered by the Soviet Stalinist regime during the "Night of the assassinated poets."

One of the most famous poems about the Holocaust was the "Todesfuge" (Death Fugue) by Paul Celan, a Jewish German-language poet born Romanian and naturalized French in 1955. The haunting aftermath of the death of his parents at an internment camp culminated with his suicide in 1970. One perceives through the fragmentation of the poem the collapse of temporal and spatial reference that conveys that a rupture has occurred and that humanity has fallen, abandoned to its own fate.

The joining of uncoupling words and the contrast of darkness and light ("black milk of daybreak") suggest this breach; all is ashes in the day as in the night. The fugue alludes to the circularity of the tragedy of existence deprived of purpose and meaning. The digging of mass graves occurs in light of God's absence and people's despair before the Absurd:

Black milk of daybreak we drink it at sundown
we drink it at noon in the morning we drink it at night
we drink and we drink
we dig a grave in the breezes there one lies unconfined
A man lives in the house he plays with the serpents he writes
he writes when dusk falls to Germany your golden hair Margarete
he writes it and steps out of doors and the stars are flashing he whistles his pack out
he whistles his Jews out in earth has them dig for a grave
he commands us strike up for the dance

Black milk of daybreak we drink you at night
we drink in the morning at noon we drink you at sundown
we drink and we drink you
A man lives in the house he plays with the serpents he writes
he writes when dusk falls to Germany your golden hair Margarete
your ashen hair Shulamith we dig a grave in the breezes there one lies unconfined. [8]

Attesting to the Shoah, the poet unveils the solitude and dispossession of humanity. Having succumbed to the angel of death, the world is here devoid of transcendence. What is needed, therefore, is an intercession. Beyond the ashes and the emptiness of existence, the poet asks us to reflect on the place and significance of the other (suggested in the juxtaposition of the golden and ashen hair). He calls on our collective consciousness to find a salutary renewed raison d'être.

RWANDA AND MULTIDIRECTIONAL MEMORIES

The Nuremberg Trial was, at least in part, the trial of Western civilization. The Holocaust raised major consequential questions for the humanities as attested in Adorno's contention about writing poetry after Auschwitz. For the leading member of the Frankfurt School, Western thought that had originated from the Renaissance and the Enlightenment had lapsed. According to this view, it was directly implicated in the rise of the totalitarian regimes that had led to the unthinkable.

Students are called here to examine history from a broader perspective. From a postcolonial outlook, Aimé Césaire equated in *Notebook of a Return to the Native Land* the barbarism of colonialism and Nazism, both illustrating a dehumanization resulting from Europe's racism. The genocidal undertaking was based in both instances on the desire to physically annihilate a people through the use of collective bureaucratic and technological resources.

It could be contended that the Armenian and Rwandan genocides were of the same nature. In this respect, Michael Rothberg's concept of multidirectional memory puts in question the relation between different traumatic memories occurring in different locales and time periods such as that of American slavery, the fate of Native Americans, and the Shoah. Rothberg contends that Holocaust memory should be explored in dialogue with others. Instead of being exclusive or the property of particular identities, they should be "subject to ongoing negotiation, cross-referencing, and borrowing."[9]

From a comparative perspective, the uniqueness of the Holocaust rests on the deliberate intention of a modern state to exterminate a people. While antisemitism was rampant for centuries, the mobilization of an entire social and administrative war machine (the Nazi Party) led the effort to round up all the Jews in Germany and its occupied countries, and subject them to a process of systematic enslavement and elimination.

What could remain after the tragic events that led to the planned, rationalized, and industrialized extermination of over six million human beings, seventy years after the liberation of the camps? While the number of survivors is declining, what endures is for students to assimilate the duty of remembering and cultivating an awakened consciousness. At the dawn of the twenty-first century, it is appropriate to ponder, with greater acuteness, what is the most proper way to give an account for these extreme events and transmit their memory.

From Auschwitz to Rwanda, Armenia to Cambodia, the stories of survivors enter the global public sphere, each testimony partaking in the construction of a collective memory. They initiate a permanent inquiry concerning the human, inhuman, and nonhuman overlap and divergence. The texts and images that result from this reflection attest to the unsayable, for future generations to grasp and to never forget.

Based on the Rwandan genocide, *The Shadow of Imana* gave Véronique Tadjo, a native of Côte d'Ivoire, and her readers the prospect of "traveling inward." She calls into question the notions of life and death, human nature, the predicament of good and evil, but also the hope that could transpire after such horror.

Tadjo was invited to visit Rwanda to bear witness to a genocide that caused the death of one million Tutsis and Hutus during one hundred days of barbaric violence. Accompanied by nine other African writers, she first painted the morbid return to daily life in Kigali, the country's capital: "Nyamata Church. Site of genocide. Plus or minus 35,000 dead. / A woman bound hand and foot. / Mukandori. Aged twenty five. Exhumed in 1997. / Home: the town of Nyamata. / Married. / Any children?"[10]

The author portrayed in a factual and sober manner the lasting haunting presence of the dead among the living: "This is not a memorial but death laid bare, exposed in all its rawness. The bones of the skeleton-corpse are disintegrating before our very eyes. The stench infects our nostrils and settles inside our lungs, contaminates our flesh, lingers in our bodies and our minds."[11]

She also recalled her encounter with the survivors whose fate was thrown in a complete state of upheaval by the genocide and ensuing war, raising questions about the justice that might one day be rendered for these atrocities. The central interrogations, however, concerned forgiveness and the potential for reconciliation among Rwandan people. How could one absolve without forgetting, how could one remember while hoping for a better future?

At the beginning of her journey, she told herself in an almost pious way: "May my eyes see, my ears hear, my mouth speak. I am not afraid of knowing. But may my mind never lose sight of what must grow with us: hope and respect for life."[12]

Students reading the novel realize how writing in this context represents both an obstacle and an opening. Words seem on the one hand incapable of transcribing the reality of atrocious violence and death; conversely, they appear to open a path toward the other, the victims of the massacre who are no longer of this world.

Through this dual perspective, Tadjo explores writing as a place of alienation and reconciliation. The power of violence and genocide is overwhelming in its irrationality. Yet in an ultimate journey toward alterity (within and beyond oneself), Tadjo's writing also aims at providing future generations a way to prevent the process of violence.

Beyond the impossible attempt to comprehend what happened within the opacity of events, Tadjo returns to a time in which the great fear of the other has been promoted. It is through this angle that the author writes to "exorcise Rwanda."

The fate of alterity is of primary importance here, for it elevates the subject to a higher degree of responsibility. In order for transcendence to be achieved, the self must be concerned for the other and find him or her within oneself. In the words of Emmanuel Levinas, "The essential nature of being is put in question [. . .] based on the face of the other."[13] Beyond Rwanda, the reader comes to realize that what happened concerns the whole of humanity, not only a people living in central Africa.

The dialogue the author initiates between the living and the dead also makes possible the representation of the "unspeakable." It brings the reader to a fictional space that journalists and historians cannot utilize: "The dead were paying regular visits to the living and when they were with them, they would ask why they had been killed. [The living replied:] Who am I to dare to cross the threshold of your pain? Who am I to disturb the course of your anger? I am the beggar in search of truth. I am the man lost in the abyss of our violence. I am he who asks you to agree to give the living another chance."[14]

At this moment, writes Tadjo, it is the dead themselves who are asking the survivors to go on living. Beyond boundaries, the author creates the possibility of a dialogue between the living and the dead. Traveling inward and calling into question human nature and the predicament of good and evil, she seeks a way to explore the dark side of humankind but also the hope that could still remain after such human horror and tragedy.

TOWARD EMPATHY AND MEANING

Anne Frank's home in Amsterdam has become, through her writing, a place of memory. More than a monument dedicated to the memory of those murdered during the Holocaust, it is one of the rare places where the conscience of each individual is inhabited by the other. The visitor comes out with a feeling of increased responsibility. She or he must strive to carry it, relentlessly, beyond the trivialities of one's own existence.

The very raison d'être of our civilization and humanity now depends on our ability to think and write about the Holocaust. What we learn about ourselves through this reflection should be shared and preserved.

First and foremost, Western civilization neither saved us from Auschwitz nor made it impossible. It seemingly succeeded in giving birth to a sophisticated system of thought, advanced knowledge, and technical capabilities, and yet ended its course in the concentration camps.

From the moment humankind created the extermination camps, it became exiled from its ideals and obedient to the law by which one could decide the annihilation of the other. After the death of God, proclaimed by Nietzsche, humanity proved that it possessed the capacity of self-destruction.

But these years of trial also conceived with the Universal Declaration of Human Rights that humanity could only redeem itself through the absolute recognition of the other. Literature attests to the philosophical and ethical effort that is required of all of us in this respect.

They demonstrated the formidable human capacity to resist the darkness and evil of Nazism. As the victims of merciless murder practices and genocidal crimes were slaughtered with machine guns in mass graves, the *Daily Telegraph* of London published a series of articles on June 25, 1942, which revealed that the Nazis had exterminated more than seven hundred thousand Polish Jews.

This information originated from a telegram received by Samuel Zygielbojm, a member of the Polish National Council in London. Distressed by the indifference of public opinion, he died by suicide the following year, writing: "May my death be a resounding cry of protest against the indifference with which the world looks at the destruction of the Jewish world, looks on, and does nothing to stop it."[15]

Samuel Zygielbojm exemplified through self-surpassing the first act of resistance that was to attest to the truth about the Holocaust, to bear witness as the world remained silent. Turning away from this atrocity was to condemn oneself to nothingness; writing about the Shoah was vital to the survival of European civilization and consciousness. He felt compelled to acknowledge what was taking place, sacrificing his very life for the cause.

It took his testimony and words of condemnation to reveal the extent of the irreparable reality. It befitted him to provide the information and inspiration that would lead to action. According to an ancient Jewish injunction, one who saves a human life also saves humanity.

The capacity for empathy and meaning is derived from the act of bearing witness in order to increase individual awareness and collective consciousness. By asking why the classics should be read, Italo Calvino referred in this respect to the role, power, and responsibility of literature before humanity. The Italian critic defined the classics as great works that never exhaust saying all they have to say. Renewed through the interests and concerns of different generations, they reveal humans' reality and place in history, generate critical discourse, and reach their ultimate relevance when they are read in the context of current moral issues.

Exercising a particular influence, the classics imprint "themselves on our imagination as unforgettable, [and hide] in the layers of memory disguised as the individual's or the collective unconscious."[16] From a historical perspective, Calvino contended that they sustain their legacy through "bearing the aura of previous interpretations, and trailing behind them the traces they have left [in the cultures, languages, and customs] through which they have passed."[17]

Put another way, "a classic is a work that relegates the noise of the present to a background hum" while its relevance persists in a present that is incompatible with it. From this perspective, while the classics seem to be at odds with our pace of life, "they help us understand who we are and the point we have reached."[18] As brief as it may have been, Zygielbojm's message achieved equal importance for the message it impressed on people's minds.

Questioning the ultimate purpose of literature and the humanities, Calvino concluded his remarks by alleging that the classics should not be read because they are "useful" but because they hold the key to entering the realm of humanity's highest aspirations: learning and creating in the context of our finitude: "If anyone objects that they are not worth all that effort, I will cite Cioran [. . .]: 'While the hemlock was being prepared, Socrates was learning a melody on the flute. What use will that be to you?' he was asked. 'At least, I will learn this melody before I die.'"[19]

The Nazis burned books and censored authors in the countries they occupied, including Walter Benjamin, John Dos Passos, Albert Einstein, and Marcel Proust. Opposed to fascistic and despotic dispositions still adopted in many countries around the world, the classics of literature and the humanities enable us to question and reinvent the world, or, according to Simone Weil, to surpass the boundaries of the written page. As such they constitute a threat to hegemonic power.

We see through the testimonies of Anne Frank and Samuel Zygielbojm how reading literature helps students question the meaning of their existence in a historical and political context. It inspires the imagination, enhances one's ability to think critically, and constitutes the foundation for all future learning. Essential to the welfare of society, it enhances empathy and a better understanding of people who are different from us. It strengthens our emotional intelligence and creates a common bond between cultures and communities.

From a quasi-spiritual point of view, according to Marcel Proust, "insofar as reading initiates us, insofar as her magic key opens the door deep inside us to the dwelling places we would not otherwise have known how to reach, its role is a salutary one."[20] This reflection that dates from 1905 was introduced in the preface to Proust's French translation of a book by John Ruskin titled *Sesame and Lilies*, first published in 1865. Proust chose the occasion of this translation to expand on John Ruskin's vision of the role of reading, and, through Marcel's memories, on his own creative process.

Ruskin's views on the subject were disseminated through lectures and texts, including "Of Kings' Treasuries" and "Of Queens' Gardens." Reading was for him at the center of a person's intellectual life, while for Proust, it was at the threshold of the spiritual life. It was an intervention that, coming from another source, was at play deep within ourselves. There were no days lived so fully than those spent with a favorite book. In these moments, the act of reading provided an intense emotion and revealed the plenitude of thought.

Reading was an occasion to converse in solitude with authors of past centuries. Proust did not believe that books should be worshipped or that they should be viewed as containing infallible truths of great minds. This way of thinking was dangerous, presenting a risk to fall into the intellectual trap of scholars whose minds, he thought, were deprived of original thinking. He rather saw reading as an opportunity for silence, which was purer than speech, and for uncovering the substances that could nourish the reader's mind and soul.

In a text that foresaw the writing of his masterpiece *In Search of Lost Time*, Proust explored what compelled the majority of readers and major authors to isolate themselves from the world. In this setting, reading and writing's magical path led to an uncovered domain of the self and others.

As such, rather than telling the story of a particular sequence of events based on the narrator's memories, Proust's novel was a reflection on literature, memory, and time. These seemingly disparate elements found themselves connected to each other when, through his experiences, the narrator, who was also the main protagonist, discovered the meaning of life in art and literature, in the last volume of the novel. *In Search of Lost Time*'s narration was progressing toward a vocation born through the remembrance of the past and longing for a synthesis, a unity of space and time, through fullness and transcendence.

WOMEN TRANSCENDING MARGINS

The writing of female authors added considerable insights within the domain of the humanities. They have introduced readers to new spaces of reflection and representation on key themes and issues pertaining to power relations and sexuality, gender inequality, and the promotion of women's rights. Specifically, writing enabled them to undermine the process of marginalization to which they were subjected. This has led, for example, to feminists and postcolonial critics taking issue with the notion of canon formation that traditionally resulted from men's political control, power structure, and patriarchal authority.

The role played by women authors has also brought about a series of challenges for the critic: How do we take into account cultural and historical differences when we write/read about women in the "global" world? Are there more legitimate voices than others at a time when globalization is redefining the concepts of identity, meta-discourse, and the rapport of each individual to the "other"?

Women have challenged, through their work, key tenets of literary history and criticism. While asserting through counterdiscourse their own new form of literary authority, they have not only redefined canon formation but also have redrawn epistemological, political, and cultural landscapes. Thus, they have dramatically transformed not only the body of literature but also the way we look at and understand literature from a political, anthropological, and cultural perspective.

By underlining the distinctive nature of their work, we uncover the extent to which women authors challenge, directly or indirectly, seemingly universally accepted totalizing structures and meta-historical principles that narrow the scope through which we assess their witness accounts. Women authors highlight the suspicion that Western feminism represents the views of a "privileged" minority, and thus runs the risk of reincorporating in its discourse a white and imperialist ideology. These inquiries demand that the critic deconstruct Western feminists' assumptions and postcolonial binary discourses apart from totalizing structures; embrace resistance, contradiction, and difference; and transcend geographic, political, cultural, critical, and ideological borders.

As an example, Gayatri Chakravorty Spivak discussed the distance one may find between the "informant's world" and the nonspecialist:

> In order to learn about Third World women and to develop a different readership, the immense heterogeneity of the field must be appreciated . . . I emphasize discontinuity, heterogeneity, and typology . . . because this work cannot by itself obliterate the problem of race and class. It will not necessarily escape the inbuilt colonialism of First World feminism toward the Third. [21]

Thus, deconstructing the Eurocentric interpretation of women authors by taking into account the northern and/or southern diversity of their creation is one of the essential paths that leads away from preassumptions and generalization toward a comprehensive approach to the female experience that can acknowledge and recognize differences within a given locale and similarities beyond.

This multiplicity of perspectives enables students to receive a more subjective and personal account of literature and feminist criticism.

The fate of women around the world is deplorable. According to UNIFEM (United Nations Development Fund for Women), which seeks to foster women's empowerment and gender equality, domestic and sexual violence against women is on the rise. More than 50 percent of women in some countries reported having been subjected to physical or sexual violence by intimate partners. In a study of female deaths in Alexandria, Egypt, 47 percent of women were killed by a relative after they had been raped by others.

Harmful traditional practices such as female genital mutilation, the trafficking of women and girls, the connection between HIV/AIDS and violence, and the violation of women's rights during and after armed conflicts continue to be the norm. Some 70 percent of the casualties in recent conflicts have been noncombatants, most of them women and children. Women are part of the battleground for those who use terror as a tactic of war; they are raped, abducted, humiliated, and made to undergo forced pregnancy, sexual abuse, and slavery.[22]

Debates among critics have centered on the extent to which, in issues pertaining to the universality of the violation of women's rights, there exists a homogenized global women's movement. Faced with this question, the concepts of "heteroglossia" and difference are essential for enabling us to examine the diversity of women's experiences in their struggle for social justice and gender equality. What is at stake is not whether women's movements exist or are needed worldwide but rather to what extent their experiences and demands converge.

One consensus among feminists has been to recognize the necessity of crossing boundaries based on race, social class, religion, and culture when addressing issues relevant to women, while emphasizing the interconnectedness of their struggle. Hence, it is what constitutes both the singularity and the diversity of the woma/en's experiences that demands a critical remapping or reconceptualization of feminism(s) that is attentive to the various and numerous aspects of the "female condition."

Reading and writing in the humanities about women authors requires students to adopt the concepts of contrapuntal and deconstructive reading, discontinuity, "heteroglossia," and difference as a method of investigation. This multifaceted approach is more exigent but also more stimulating for them. It is based on the specificity of the women's experiences, wherever they might be. Here students must break boundaries and stereotypes and go beyond a homogenized form of feminism determined by Western ideology.

Taking into account the ambivalent nature of "postcolonial" and "feminist" theories by returning to the scene of writing whereby the text opens itself to the breaking down of boundaries and the emergence of new subjectivities, students can explore how writing and reading become a form of empowerment through which authors and readers deconstruct dominant political/cultural or critical/theoretical discourses while affirming their own subjectivity.

Such a "real-life" exploration of this vast array of women's expression in the domain of comparative cultural studies enables students to bring to light the dialogue among women authors from different countries and cultural traditions. They also examine how specific themes and motifs such as the construction of identity, the tension between tradition and modernity, and the struggle of women with oppression and patriarchy are introduced, resolved, and/or unsettled.

These questions go to the heart of the purpose of literature itself which, as Françoise Lionnet contends, "Allows us to enter into the subjective processes of writers and their characters, [. . .] to better understand the unique perspectives of subjects who are agents of transformation and hybridization in their own narratives, as opposed to being the objects of knowledge as in the discourse of social science."[23]

This interpretation of women authors also points "the way back to a new/ old concept: humanism, a word that feminists of different stripes are beginning to revalorize, or to borrow Evelyn Accad's more precise formulation, a 'femihumanism,' a non-separatist feminism committed to bringing about a pluralistic society based on the rejection of oppression and domination, whether globally or locally."[24]

Extending the margins of feminism and postcolonialism, the authors enunciate critical issues; they invite students to interrogate the text and to broaden their knowledge of women's cross-cultural and subjective experience. These literary works address interrelated themes and topics that complement and overlap each other: the formation of hybrid and feminine identity, border crossing, the place of women in society, violence and taboos, women's sexuality, the influence and/or rejection of the colonial past, and the power conflicts along the lines of class and gender.

Redefining the political dimension of feminist theory and practice, students uncover how women authors raise awareness of power imbalances in their respective society, resist a system that has suppressed and excluded them legally, socially, and culturally throughout history, and cut through the notions of demarcation between national cultures. Women escape the masculinist's discourse and structuring rules by countering the dominating collective order.

In this framework, language is not marked by exclusion but reconciliation and the emergence of a literature detached of all national paradigms, freed of all forms of power other than the one of imagination, having as sole border the one of the mind and spirit.

CONTRAPUNTAL READINGS

Transcending disciplinary boundaries (from literature, art, sociology, anthro-pology, to political science), Edward Said epitomized the humanities' ability to promote and enable interdisciplinary thinking and call to reconcile critical activity and political commitment. He inscribed the study of literature in a cultural and historical context rather than in abstract theory, searching for political meaning in artistic and literary practice. In a world "controlled by big business and money," music represented an opportunity for acculturation and a resistance to the reduction of everything to the status of merchandise.

In *Parallels and Paradoxes*, Said's peer and friend, the pianist and con-ductor Daniel Barenboim, also reflected on the nature and significance of music performance and the similarities it shares with political and ethical actions. One could discern, he claimed, through the aims of a committed artist or musician the attempts to build bridges between different genres and cultures and toward the discovery of the other.

Bringing together young people from different Middle Eastern countries, the West–Eastern Divan Orchestra that he conducted revealed the power of music to open the ears, minds, and hearts of listeners and performers.

> What seemed extraordinary to me was how much ignorance there was about the other. The Israeli kids could not imagine that there are people in Damascus and Amman and Cairo who can actually play violin and viola. [. . .] One of the Syrian kids told me that he had never met an Israeli before [. . .]. This same boy found himself sharing a music stand with an Israeli cellist. They were trying to play the same note, to play with the same dynamic, with the same stroke of the bow, with the same sound, with the same expression. It is as simple as that. [. . .] Having achieved that one note, they already can't look at each other the same way, because they have shared a common experience.[25]

Illustrative of a democratic art form, music enables one to hear more than one voice at a time, to express oneself, to be heard and participate in the communal performance of masterpieces.

Like Said, Daniel Barenboim interwove the pace of harmonic progression with the unfolding of the political process. He considered the extent to which both could change the reality of millions in diverse cultures and societies. One could conceive, he asserted, the makeup of a nation as a musical score, its politicians as interpreters who must constantly act and react according to specific frames of reference. Likewise, a democracy could be envisioned as a collectively composed symphony.

The West–Eastern Divan Orchestra promoted an exchange and dialogue between people's intellect, emotion, and intuition. What was beneficial to individuals or groups was also essential to nations. The inclusion of all parties, whether in the realm of the arts or international diplomacy, aimed at ensuring cohesiveness and harmony and creating the necessary conditions for cooperation. While politicians were ineffectual in resolving issues, music made people "feel nearer to each other, and that is all."[26]

The universal metaphysical language of music became the means through which young people of different origins and beliefs imagined the contours of a new political reality. The realm of sound was capable of inspiring each individual to move from concern solely for one's own existence to that of other human beings. If the orchestra could not by itself bring peace, it could create the conditions for understanding without which it was impossible to speak about peace, to listen and learn about each other's story. Barenboim underscored in this respect the transcendent dimension and power of music:

> Music is more than a mirror of life; it is enriched by the metaphysical dimension of sound, which gives it the possibility to transcend physical, human limitations. In the world of sound, even death is not necessarily final [. . .]. We must never stop asking ourselves what exactly the content of music is. [. . .] It cannot be defined as having merely a mathematical, a poetic, or a sensual content. It is all those things and much more. It has to do with the condition of being human, since the music is written and performed by human beings who express their innermost thoughts, feelings, impressions, and observations.[27]

Barenboim and Said show us how music goes beyond its artistic prerogative by bringing people together. Similarly to contrapuntal reading, it transcends margins and requires its students to distance themselves from dominant discourses and be emancipated from given ideological presuppositions. Arguing that music possesses a unique "sense of displacement," they contend that its study is "one of the best ways to learn about human nature."[28]

Reading against the grain, which has fed into the analysis of feminist discourse, queer theory, and Derrida's deconstruction of presence, as well as minority literatures and subaltern studies, partakes not only in elaborating diverse approaches to texts but also in forging local and global visions of a transformed social and political reality.

In the context of current world events, the humanities take on through the role of the West–Eastern Divan Orchestra what is perhaps their greatest unrecognized importance and value: to cross boundaries, expand the possibility for argumentation and dialogue, question one's assumptions and beliefs, and, within and beyond difference, acknowledge people's humanity.

Inspired by music's power of displacement, Edward Said associated being both an intellectual and also a human being with the ability to wander without a fixed territorial base or a speculative theoretical anchor. Through a form of nomadism, he promoted a critique that aimed at transcending academic disciplines but also the self/other dichotomies. Recreative and personal, the works of essayists and pianists often called for a renewed critical reading and interpretation.

Said led students to make comparisons and draw analogies moving from one field or domain to another. By exploring literary and artistic works of different origins, one escapes from the self to reach what he names the realm of worldliness, a feeling one possesses of belonging to planet Earth. From that point on, the artistic, cultural, and political interplay strengthened and broadened the ethical dimension he perceived was necessary to transform the global human experience.

Beyond geographic boundaries and the fixity of theoretical systems that discount the relation binding literary and artistic works to society and the world, students as readers and listeners maintain a critical distance from preconceived structures and dogmas to open themselves and be engaged with the concrete issues and challenges of our time.

Said believed that marginality and "homelessness" should end through our making, so that more people victims of racial, class, or gender prejudice may enjoy the benefits of what has long been denied to them: human rights and dignity. The condition of exile was for him a source of grief and suffering: "It is the unhealable rift forced between a human being and native place, between the self and its true home."[29]

The articles on Egypt ("Egyptian Rites" and "Cairo and Alexandria") were descriptive of the foreign condition that embodied, in Said's case, the posture of an individual neither American Palestinian nor American of Palestinian origin, but Palestinian, having migrated to Egypt into a francophone community. By contrast, the concept of the "exotic" conveyed blindness and the inability to move "out of oneself." It implied a static definition of alterity and, broadly speaking, alluded to the condescendence of Western discourse toward "the Orient."

While exile (antonymous to "exotic") from one's homeland brought suffering, it also provided a critical distance and detachment from predefined identity and preconceived orthodoxy. Said was "between worlds," and he reaffirmed through this posture the necessity of engagement on the part of students and academics who needed to move from the university to the world, he thought, in order to nurture in them a sense of intellectual vocation: "Exile in life led outside habitual order. It is nomadic, decentered, contrapuntal."[30]

In our societies marked by technology, economic interests, and media discourse devoid of critical perspectives, Said and Barenboim called on us to be thinkers in the world whose critical task would be to consider people of different cultures and origins under the banner of humanity beyond geographical or religious boundaries.

Being in the world requires scholars, students, and the public at large to reflect about oneself and others through the study of the literary, musical, and artistic narratives that demand reflection upon the purpose and proper means of humanity's existence. The task of the artist, writer, and critic is political in this respect. It demands a consideration of texts and compositions as events that could affect people and society, help understand the human experience, and alter through exchange and dialogue the course of history.

The author and musician underscored the hybridization of all cultures and knowledge that do not exist in isolation. There was no essence of the West or the Orient as such, Said contended, but diverse interwoven forms of experiences and expressions. In this instance, liberal education exposes the limits of totality and enables students to reach beyond their own finite presence. What they uncover is a sense of infinite responsibility toward the other.

NOTES

1. Sherry Turkle, *Reclaiming Conversation: The Power of Talk in a Digital Age* (New York: Penguin Press, 2015).

2. "The Reading Agency," *Arts Council England*, 2016, http://readingagency.org.uk.

3. John Armstrong, "The School of Life," *The School of Life*, 2016, www.theschooloflife.com.

4. Emanuele Castano and David Comer Kidd, "Reading Literary Fiction Improves Theory of Mind," Science , October 2013.

5. Marianne Hirsch, "Surviving Images: Holocaust Photographs and the Work of Postmemory," Yale Journal of Criticism 14, no. 1 (2001): 10.

6. Paul Ricoeur, *Memory, History, Forgetting* (Chicago: University of Chicago Press, 2006), 5–6.

7. Elie Wiesel, Night, translated by Marion Wiesel (New York: Hill and Wang, 2006), 34.

8. Paul Celan, "Death Fugue," in *Art from the Ashes: A Holocaust Anthology*, edited by Lawrence L. Langer (New York: Oxford University Press, 1995), 601.

9. Michael Rothberg, *Multidirectional Memory: Remembering the Holocaust in the Age of Decolonization* (Stanford, CA: Stanford University Press, 2009), 3.

10. Véronique Tadjo, *The Shadow of Imana*, translated by Véronique Wakerley (Oxford: Heinemann, 2002), 11.

11. Tadjo, *The Shadow of Imana*, 12.

12. Tadjo, *The Shadow of Imana*, 10.

13. Emmanuel Levinas, *Entre Nous: On Thinking-of-the-Other* (New York: Columbia University Press, 1998), 147.

14. Tadjo, *The Shadow of Imana*, 43.

15. Samuel Totten and Paul R. Bartrop, eds., *Dictionary of Genocide*, Volume 2 (Westport, CT: Greenwood Press, 2008), 486.

16. Italo Calvino, *Why Read the Classics?* translated by Martin McLaughlin (New York: Vintage Books, 2001), 4.

17. Calvino, *Why Read the Classics?* 5.

18. Calvino, *Why Read the Classics?* 8–9.

19. Calvino, *Why Read the Classics?* 9.

20. Marcel Proust, "On Reading," *Marcel Proust and John Ruskin on Reading*, foreword by Eric Karpeles (London: Hesperus Press, 2011), 27.

21. Gayatri Chakaravorty Spivak, "French Feminism in an International Frame" in Sandra Kemp, *Feminisms* (Oxford: Oxford University Press, 1997), 53–54.

22. "Facts and Figures: Ending Violence against Women." *UNICEF*, February 2016, http://www.unwomen.org/en/what-we-do/ending-violence-against-women/facts-and-figures.

23. Françoise Lionnet, ed., *Postcolonial Subjects: Francophone Women Authors* (Minneapolis: University of Minnesota Press, 1996), 323.

24. Lionnet, *Postcolonial Subjects*, 331.

25. Daniel Barenboim and Edward W. Said, *Parallels and Paradoxes* (New York: Pantheon Books, 2002), 10.

26. Barenboim and Said, *Parallels and Paradoxes*, 11.

27. Daniel Barenboim, *Music Quickens Time* (London: Verso, 2008), 9–10.

28. Barenboim and Said, *Parallels and Paradoxes*, 24–25.

29. Edward W. Said, *Reflections on Exile* (Cambridge: Harvard University Press, 2000), 178.

30. Said, *Reflections on Exile*, 186.

Bibliography

Abbot, Porter H. *The Cambridge Introduction to Narrative.* Cambridge: Cambridge University Press, 2008.

Adler, Mortimer J. *A Guidebook to Learning: For the Lifelong Pursuit of Wisdom.* New York: MacMillian, 1986.

_____. *Reforming Education: The Opening of the American Mind.* New York: Macmillan, 1990.

Adorno, Theodor. *Can One Live after Auschwitz? A Philosophical Reader.* Edited by Rolf Tiedemann. Stanford, CA: Stanford University Press, 2003.

Aldama, Frederick Luis. *Why the Humanities Matter: A Commonsense Approach.* Austin: University of Texas Press, 2008.

Alexander, Jacqui, and Chandra Talpade Mohanty, ed. *Feminist Genealogies, Colonial Legacies, Democratic Futures.* London: Routledge, 2012.

Altbach, Philip G., Patricia J. Gumport, Robert O. Berdahl. *American Higher Education in the Twenty-First Century: Social, Political and Economic Challenges.* Baltimore: Johns Hopkins University Press, 2011.

Altman, Rick. *A Theory of Narrative.* New York: Columbia University Press, 2008.

Appiah, Kwame Anthony. *Experiments in Ethics.* Cambridge, MA: Harvard University Press, 2010.

Apple, Michael W. *Education and Power.* London: Routledge, 2011.

Arendt, Hannah. *Between Past and Future.* New York: Penguin Classics, 2006.

_____. *Eichmann in Jerusalem: A Report on the Banality of Evil.* New York: Penguin Classics, 2006.

_____. *The Origins of Totalitarianism.* New York: Harcourt, 1973.

Aristotle. *Nicomachean Ethics.* Translated by Robert C. Bartlett and Susan D. Collins. Chicago: University of Chicago Press, 2011.

_____. *Poetics.* Translated by Anthony Kenny. New York: Oxford University Press, 2013.

_____. *Politics.* Translated by Carnes Lord. Chicago: University of Chicago Press, 2013.

Arnason, H. H., and Elizabeth C. Mansfield. *History of Modern Art.* New York: Pearson, 2009.

Arnold, Matthew. *Culture and Anarchy.* New York: Oxford University Press, 2009.

_____. "Literature and Science." The Rede Lecture. *The Nineteenth Century*, August 1882.

Auerbach, Erich. *Mimesis: The Representation of Reality in Western Culture.* Translated by Willard R. Trask. Princeton, NJ: Princeton University Press, 2003.

Ayers, Edward L. "Where the Humanities Live." *Daedalus* 138, no. 1 (2009): 24–34.

Badmington, Neil. *Posthumanism.* New York: Palgrave MacMillan, 2000.

Ball, Philip. *The Music Instinct: How Music Works and Why We Can't Do Without It.* Oxford: Oxford University Press, 2012.

Bardhan, Kalpana, ed. *The Oxford India Anthology of Bengali Literature.* New Delhi: Oxford University Press, 2010.

Barenboim, Daniel. *Music Quickens Time.* London: Verso, 2008.

Barenboim, Daniel, and Edward W. Said. *Parallels and Paradoxes.* New York: Pantheon Books, 2002.

Barnes, Colin, and Geof Mercer. *Exploring Disability.* Cambridge, Polity Press, 2010.

Barrow, John D. *The Limits of Science and the Science of Limits.* New York: Oxford University Press, 1998.

Barthes, Roland. *Camera Lucida: Reflections on Photography.* Translated by Richard Howard. New York: Hill and Wang, 2010.

_____. *Image-Music-Text.* Translated by Stephen Hearth. New York: Hill and Wang, 1978.

Bartleft, Jennifer, Sheila Black, and Michael Northen, ed. *Beauty Is a Verb: The New Poetry of Disability.* El Paso, TX: Cinco Puntos Press, 2011.

Baruah, Bipasha. *Women and Property in Urban India.* Vancouver: University of British Columbia, 2010.

Baudrillard, Jean. *Simulacra and Simulacrum.* Translated by Sheila Glaser. Ann Arbor: University of Michigan Press, 1994.

Bauerlein, Mark. *The Dumbest Generation: How the Digital Age Stupefies Young Americans and Jeopardizes Our Future.* New York: Penguin Books, 2008.

_____. "How Theory Damaged the Humanities." *Chronicle of Higher Education Commentary,* 2008.

Bauerlein, Mark, and Ellen Grantham. *National Endowment for the Arts: A History.* Washington, DC: National Endowment for the Arts, 2009.

Bauman, Zygmunt. *Postmodern Ethics.* Oxford: Blackwell Publishers, 1993.

Beauvoir de, Simone. *The Second Sex.* Translated by Constance Borde and Sheila Molovany-Chevallier. New York: First Vintage Books, 2011.

Benjamin, Walter. *Illuminations.* Edited by Hannah Arendt. New York: Schoken Books, 1969.

_____. *The Work of Art in the Age of Its Technological Reproducibility, and Other Writings on Media.* New York: Belknap Press, 2008.

Bennett, Bill. *To Reclaim a Legacy: A Report on the Humanities in Higher Education.* Washington, DC: Department of Education, 1984.

Bennett, John B. *Academic Life: Hospitality, Ethics, and Spirituality.* Bolton, MA: Anker Publishing Company, 2003.

Berg Olsen, Jan Kyrre, Evan Selinger, and Soren Riis, ed. *New Waves in Philosophy of Technology.* New York: Palgrave McMillan, 2009.

Berlo, Janet Catherine, and Ruth B. Phillips. *Native North American Art.* Oxford: Oxford University Press, 1998.

Bernstein, Leonard. *The Unanswered Questions: Six Talks at Harvard.* Cambridge, MA: Harvard University Press, 1981.

Berry, David M., ed. *Understanding Digital Humanities.* New York: McMillan Palgrave, 2012.

Bérubé, Michael. "How We Got Here." Presidential Address. *Publication of the Modern Language Association of America* 128, no. 3 (2013).

_____. "The Humanities, Unraveled." *The Chronicle Review,* February 2013.

Bérubé, Michael, and Cary Nelson, ed. *Higher Education under Fire.* New York: Routledge, 1994.

Bhabha, Homi. *The Location of Culture.* London: Routledge, 1994.

Blanchot, Maurice. *The Infinite Conversation.* Translated by Susan Hanson. Minneapolis: University of Minnesota Press, 1993.

Bloom, Allan. *The Closing of the American Mind: How High Education Has Failed Democracy and Impoverished the Souls of Today's Students.* New York: Simon and Schuster, 1987.

Bloom, Harold. *How to Read and Why.* New York: Scribner, 2001.

Bod, Rens, Jaap Maat, and Thijs Weststeijn, ed. *The Making of the Humanities,* Vols. 1–2, Amsterdam: Amsterdam University Press, 2011, 2013.

Bok, Derek. *Higher Education in America.* Princeton, NJ: Princeton University Press, 2013.

_____. *Universities in the Marketplace: The Commercialization of Higher Education.* Princeton, NJ: Princeton University Press, 2004.

Bonnefoy, Yves. *The Act and the Place of Poetry*. Edited and with an Introduction by John T. Naughton. Chicago: University of Chicago Press, 1989.

Bourdieu, Pierre. *The Field of Cultural Production. Essays on Art and Literature*. Edited and Introduced by Randall Johnson. New York: Columbia University Press, 1993.

_____. *Homo Academicus*. Translated by Peter Collier. Stanford, CA: Stanford University Press, 1990.

_____. *The Social Structures of the Economy*. Translated by Chris Turner. Cambridge: Polity Press, 2005.

Bowers, Chet A. *Let Them Eat Data: How Computers Affect Education, Cultural Diversity, and the Prospects of Ecological Sustainability*. Athens: University of Georgia Press, 2000.

Bowman, Wayne D. *Philosophical Perspectives on Music*. Oxford: Oxford University Press, 1998.

Bradley, Arthur. *Originary Technicity: The Theory of Technology from Marx to Derrida*. London: Palgrave Macmillan, 2011.

Braidotti, Rosi. *The Posthuman*. Cambridge: Polity Press, 2013.

Brooks, Peter, ed. *The Humanities and Public Life*. New York: Fordham University Press, 2014.

Brooks, Peter, Jonathan Culler, Marjorie Garber, E. Ann Kaplan, George Levine, Katharine R. Stimpson. *Speaking for the Humanities*. New York: American Council of Learned Societies, Occasional Paper No. 7, 1989.

Bruni, Frank. "It's a College, Not a Cloister." *New York Times*, February 2012.

Buchholz, Elke Linda, Susanne Kaeppele, and Karoline Hille, ed. *Art: A World History*. New York: Abrams, 2007.

Buell, Lawrence. *The Future of Environmental Criticism: Environmental Crisis and Literary Imagination*. Oxford: Oxford University Press, 2005.

Bundrick, Sheramy D. *Music and Image in Classical Athens*. Cambridge: Cambridge University Press, 2005.

Butler, Judith. *Dispossession: The Performative in the Political: Conversations with Athena Athanasiou*. Cambridge: Polity Press, 2013.

_____. *Gender Trouble: Feminism and the Subversion of Identity*. London: Routledge, 2006.

Cahn, Steven M., and Peter Markie. *Ethics: History, Theory, and Contemporary Issues*. New York: Oxford University Press, 2011.

Calvino, Italo. *Why Read the Classics?* Translated by Martin McLaughlin. New York: Vintage Books, 2001.

Campbell, Don, and Alex Doman. *Healing at the Speed of Sound: How What We Hear Transforms Our Brains and Our Lives*. New York: Penguin, 2012.

Campbell, Joseph. *The Power of Myth*. New York: Anchor Books, 1991.

Camus, Albert. *The Myth of Sisyphus and Other Essays*. Translated by Justin O'Brien. New York: Vintage, 1991.

Carnochan, W. B. *The Battleground of the Curriculum: Liberal Education and American Experience*. Stanford, CA: Stanford University Press, 1994.

Carson, Ronald A., Chester R. Burns, and Thomas R. Cole, ed. *Practicing the Medical Humanities: Engaging Physicians and Patients*. Hagerstown: University Publishing Group, 2003.

Carter, Jimmy. *A Call to Action: Women, Religion, Violence, and Power*. New York: Simon and Schuster, 2014.

Castano, Emanuele, and David Comer Kidd. "Reading Literary Fiction Improves Theory of Mind." *Science*, October 2013.

Caws, Mary Ann, ed. *The Yale Anthology of Twentieth-Century French Poetry*. New Haven, CT: Yale University Press, 2004.

Certeau, Michel de. *The Practice of Everyday Life*. Translated by Steven Rendall. Berkeley: University of California Press, 1984.

Cervantes, Miguel de. *Don Quixote*. Translated by Tobias Smollett. New York: Barnes & Noble Classics, 2004.

Césaire, Aimé. *Discourse on Colonialism*. Translated by Joan Pinkham. New York: Monthly Review Press, 2001.

Charle, Christophe, and Jacques Verger. *Histoire des universités.* Paris: Presses Universitaires de France, 1994.

Cheney, Lynne V. *Humanities in America: A Report to the President, the Congress, and the American People.* Washington, DC: National Endowment for the Humanities, 1988.

Cicero, Marcus Tullius. *Selected Works.* Translated with an Introduction by Michael Grant. New York: Penguin Books, 1971.

Citton, Yves. *L'avenir des humanités. Économie de la connaissance ou cultures de l'interprétation.* Paris: Éditions la Découverte, 2010.

Clark, J. R., and Dwight R. Lee. "Markets and Morality." *Cato Journal* 31, no 1 (Winter 2011).

Clark, T. J. *Picasso and Truth: From Cubism to Guernica.* Princeton, NJ: Princeton University Press, 2013.

————. *The Sight of Death: An Experiment in Art Writing.* New Haven, CT: Yale University Press, 2008.

Clark, Timothy. *The Cambridge Introduction to Literature and the Environment.* Cambridge: Cambridge University Press, 2011.

Clarke, Bruce. *Posthuman Metamorphosis: Narrative and Systems.* New York: Fordham University Press, 2008.

Clover, Joshua. "Value, Theory, Crisis." *PMLA* 127, no. 1 (2012): 107–14.

Cohen, Daniel. *Homo Economicus: The (Lost) Prophet of Modern Times.* Cambridge: Polity Press, 2014.

Cohen, Daniel, and Marcelo Soto. "Growth and Human Capital: Good Data, Good Results." *Journal of Economic Growth* 12 (2007): 51–76.

Cohen, Patricia. "In Tough Times, the Humanities Must Justify Their Worth." *New York Times*, February 24, 2009.

Cohen, Tom, ed. *Jacques Derrida and the Humanities: A Critical Reader.* New York: Cambridge University Press, 2001.

Colby, Anne, Elizabeth Beaumont, Thomas Ehrlich, and Josh Corngold. *Educating for Democracy: Preparing Undergraduates for Responsible Political Engagement.* Stanford, CA: The Carnegie Foundation for the Advancement of Teaching, 2007.

Colby, Anne, Jonathan R. Dolle, Thomas Ehrlich, and William M. Sullivan. *Rethinking Undergraduate Business Education.* Stanford: The Carnegie Foundation for the Advancement of Teaching, 2011.

Colby, Anne, Thomas Ehrlich, Elizabeth Beaumont, and Jason Stephens. *Educating Citizens: Preparing America's Undergraduates for Lives of Moral and Civic Responsibility.* Stanford: The Carnegie Foundation for the Advancement of Teaching, 2010.

Collini, Stefan. *What Are the Universities For?* New York: Penguin, 2012.

Compagnon, Antoine. *Literature, Theory, and Common Sense.* Translated by Carol Cosman. Princeton, NJ: Princeton University Press, 2004.

Comte-Sponville, André. *Le capitalisme est-il moral?* Paris: Albin Michel, 2009.

Cooper, David D. *Learning in the Plural: Essays on the Humanities and Public Life.* East Lansing: Michigan State University Press, 2014.

Coplan, Amy, and Peter Goldie. *Empathy: Philosophical and Psychological Perspectives.* Oxford: Oxford University Press, 2014.

Copland, Aaron. *What to Listen For in Music.* New York: New American Library, 2009.

Cottom, Daniel. *Why Education Is Useless.* Philadelphia: University of Pennsylvania Press, 2003.

Coulter, David, and John R. Wiens, ed. *Why Do We Educate? Renewing the Conversation.* Malden, MA: Blackwell Publishing, 2008.

Coupe, Laurence, ed. *The Green Studies Reader: From Romanticism to Ecocriticism.* London: Routledge, 2000.

Critchley, Simon. *The Ethics of Deconstruction: Derrida and Lévinas.* Edinburgh: Edinburgh University Press, 2014.

Curren, Randall, ed. *Philosophy of Education. An Anthology.* Malden, MA: Blackwell Publishing, 2007.

Danto, Arthur C. *The Abuse of Beauty: Aesthetics and the Concept of Art.* New York: Open Court, 2003.

_____. *After the End of Art*. Princeton, NJ: Princeton University Press, 1998.

_____. *What Art Is*. New Haven, CT: Yale University Press, 2014.

Darwin, Charles. *The Origin of Species*. New York: Bantam Classics, 1999.

Dasgupta, Ajit K. *Gandhi's Economic Thought*. London: Routledge, 1996.

Davidson, Cathy N. "Humanities 2.0: Promise, Perils, Predictions. The Role of the Humanities in the Information Age." *PMLA* 123, no. 3 (2008): 707–17.

Davis, Lennard J., ed. *The Disability Studies Reader*. New York: Routledge, 2013.

Da Vinci, Leonardo. *Notebooks*. Edited with an Introduction and Notes by Thereza Wells. New York: Oxford University Press, 2008.

_____. *Trattato Della Pittura*. Charleston, SC: Nabu Press, 2012.

De Bolla, Peter. *Art Matters*. Cambridge, MA: Harvard University Press, 2001.

De Koninck, Thomas. *La nouvelle ignorance et le problème de la culture*. Paris: Presses Universitaires de France, 2000.

Delanty, Gerard. *The Cosmopolitan Imagination: The Renewal of Critical Social Theory*. Cambridge: Cambridge University Press, 2009.

Delbanco, Andrew. *College: What It Was, Is, and Should Be*. Princeton, NJ: Princeton University Press, 2012.

Deleuze, Gilles, and Félix Guattari. *A Thousand Plateaus: Capitalism and Schizophrenia*. Translated and Foreword by Brian Massumi. Minneapolis: University of Minnesota Press, 1987.

Del Sarto, Ana, Alicia Rios, and Abril Trigo, ed. *The Latin American Cultural Studies Reader*. Durham, NC: Duke University Press, 2004.

Derek, Allan. *Art and Time*. Newcastle: Cambridge Scholars Publishing, 2013.

Derrida, Jacques. *The Animal That Therefore I Am*. Translated by David Willis. New York: Fordham University Press, 2008.

_____. *Of Grammatology*. Translated by Gayatri Chakravorty Spivak. Baltimore: Johns Hopkins University Press, 1997.

_____. *Specters of Marx: The State of the Debt, the Work of Mourning, and the New International*. Translated by Peggy Kamuf. London: Routledge, 1994.

_____. *Writing and Difference*. Translated by Alan Bass. London: Routledge, 2001.

Descartes, René. *Discourse on Method and Related Writings*. New York: Penguin Classics, 1999.

DeShazer, Mary K. *Longman Anthology of Women's Literature*. New York: Longman, 2000.

Dewey, John. *Art as Experience*. New York: Perigee Book, 1980.

_____. *Democracy and Education: An Introduction to the Philosophy of Education*. New York: Simon and Brown, 2012.

_____. *Experience and Education*. New York: Free Press, 1997.

DeWilde, Michael. "The Business of the Humanities." *Chronicle of Higher Education*, July 1, 2005.

Dimitriadis, Greg, and George Kamberelis. *Theory for Education*. London: Routledge, 2006.

Diop, Cheikh Anta. *Civilization or Barbarism: An Authentic Anthropology*. Translated by Yaa-Lengi Meema Ngemi. Chicago: Chicago Review Press, 1991.

Donoghue, Denis, ed. *The Practice of Reading*. New Haven, CT: Yale University Press, 2000.

_____. "What Humanists Do." *Daedalus: The Journal of the American Academy of Arts & Sciences* 143, no. 1 (Winter 2014).

Donoghue, Frank. *The Last Professors: The Corporate University and the Fate of the Humanities*. New York: Fordham University Press, 2008.

_____. "Can the Humanities Survive the 21st Century?" *Chronicle of Higher Education*, September 5, 2010.

Dostoyevsky, Fyodor. *The Brothers Karamazov*. Translated by Richard Pevear and Larissa Volokhonsky. New York: Farrar, Straus and Giroux, 2002.

Du Bois, W. E. B. *The Souls of Black Folk*. Oakland, CA: Eucalyptus Press, 2013.

Duby, Georges, and Jean-Luc Daval. *Sculpture: From Antiquity to the Present Day, 2 vols*. Köln: Taschen Books, 2010.

Dupré, John. *Human Nature and the Limits of Science*. Oxford: Oxford University Press, 2002.

Durant, Will, and Ariel Durant. *The Lessons of History*. New York: Simon & Schuster, 2010.

Durkheim, Émile. *Moral Education: A Study in the Theory and Application of the Sociology of Education.* New York: Free Press, 1961.

Eagleton, Terry. *After Theory.* New York: Basic Books, 2004.

_____. *The Illusions of Postmodernism.* Oxford: Blackwell, 1996.

_____. Review of *The Trouble with Principle* by Stanley Fish, *London Review of Books*, Vol. 22, no. 5 (March 2000).

Eco, Umberto. *History of Beauty.* Milan: Rizzoli, 2010.

_____. *The Limits of Interpretation.* Bloomington: Indiana University Press, 1991.

Edmundson, Mark. *The Academy Writes Back.* New York: Penguin Books, 1993.

Egan, Kieran. *The Future of Education: Reimagining our Schools from the Ground Up.* New Haven, CT: Yale University Press, 2004.

Egéa-Kuehne, Denise, ed. *Lévinas and Education.* London: Routledge, 2008.

Einstein, Albert. *The Collected Papers of Albert Einstein.* Vol. 2, *The Swiss Years: Writings, 1900–1909.* Translated by Anna Beck. Princeton, NJ: Princeton University Press, 1989.

_____. *Ideas and Opinions.* New York: The Modern Library, 1994.

Eisenhower, Dwight. "Farewell Address to the Nation." January 17, 1961.

Elliot, David J. *Music Matters: A New Philosophy of Music Education.* Oxford: Oxford University Press, 1995.

Ellul, Jacques. *The Technological Society.* Translated by John Wilkinson. New York: Vintage Books, 1964.

Emerson, Ralph Waldo. *The Essential Writings.* Introduction by Mary Oliver. New York: Random House, 2000.

Epstein, Mikhail. *The Transformative Humanities: A Manifesto.* New York: Bloomsbury, 2012.

Erasmus, Desiderius. *Education of a Christian Prince.* Translated by Lester K. Born. New York: Columbia University Press, 1968.

Erevelles, Nirmala. *Disability and Difference in Global Contexts: Enabling a Transformative Body Politic.* New York: Palgrave McMillan, 2011.

Erfani, Farhang, ed. *Paul Ricoeur: Honoring and Continuing the Work.* Lanham, MD: Lexington Books, 2011.

Evans, Martyn, and Ilora G. Finlay, ed. *Medical Humanities.* London: BMJ Books, 2001.

Fadiman, Clifton, John S. Major, and Katharine Washburn, ed. *World Poetry: An Anthology of Verse from Antiquity to Our Time.* New York: W. W. Norton & Company, 2000.

Fairchild Ruggles, D., ed. *Islamic Art and Visual Culture: An Anthology of Sources.* Malden, MA: Wiley-Blackwell, 2011.

Fall, N'Goné, and Jean-Loup Pivin, ed. *An Anthology of African Art: The Twentieth-Century.* New York: Distributed Art Publishers, 2002.

Fara, Patricia. *Science: A Four Thousand Year History.* Oxford: Oxford University Press, 2010.

Felner, Mira, and Claudia Orenstein. *The World of Theatre: Tradition and Innovation.* New York: Pearson, 2005.

Fendrich, Laurie. "The Humanities Have No Purpose." *Chronicle of Higher Education*, March 2009.

Ferber, Marianne A., and Julie A. Nelson. *Feminist Economics Today: Beyond Economic Man.* Chicago: University of Chicago Press, 2003.

Ferrall, Victor E. *Liberal Arts at the Brink.* Cambridge, MA: Harvard University Press, 2011.

Ferry, Luc. *A Brief History of Thought: A Philosophical Guide to Living.* Translated by Theo Cuffe. New York: Harper Perennial, 2011.

_____. *The Wisdom of the Myths: How Greek Mythology Can Change Your Life.* Translated by Theo Cuffe. New York: Harper Perennial, 2014.

Feyerabend, Paul K. *The Tyranny of Science.* Cambridge: Polity Press, 2011.

Fish, Stanley. "A Case for the Humanities Not Made." *New York Times*, June 2013.

_____. *Save the World on your Own Time.* New York: Oxford University Press, 2008.

_____. "Will the Humanities Save Us?" Opinionator, *New York Times*, January 6, 2008.

Foerster, Norman. *The Humanities and the Common Man: The Democratic Role of the State Universities.* Chapel Hill: The University of North Carolina Press, 1946.

Foucault, Michel. *The Order of Things: An Archeology of the Human Sciences.* New York: Vintage Books, 1995.

Franke, Richard J. "The Power of the Humanities and a Challenge to Humanists." *Daedalus* 138, no. 1 (Winter 2009): 13–23.

Freire, Paulo. *Education for Critical Consciousness.* London: Bloomsbury, 2013.

_____. *Pedagogy of Freedom: Ethics, Democracy, and Civic Courage.* Translated by Patrick Clarke. Lanham, MD: Rowman & Littlefield Publishers, 2001.

_____. *Pedagogy of the Oppressed.* New York: Bloomsbury Publishing, 2000.

Freud, Sigmund. *Civilization and Its Discontents.* Mansfield Centre, CT: Martino Books, 2011.

_____. *The Freud Reader.* Edited by Peter Gay. New York: W. W. Norton & Company, 1995.

Fullbrook, Edward, ed. *A Guide to What's Wrong with Economics.* London: Anthem Press, 2004.

Fynsk, Christopher. *The Claim of Language: A Case for the Humanities.* Minneapolis: University of Minnesota Press, 2004.

Gandhi, Leela. *Postcolonial Theory: A Critical Introduction.* New York: Columbia University Press, 1998.

Gandhi, Mohandas Karamchand (Mahatma). *Autobiography: The Story of My Experiments with Truth.* New York: CreateSpace Independent Publishing Platform, 2012.

Garber, Marjorie. *Academic Instincts.* Princeton, NJ: Princeton University Press, 2003.

Gardner, Howard. *Frames of Mind: The Theory of Multiple Intelligences.* New York: Basic Books, 2011.

Garrard, Greg. *Ecocriticism.* London: Routledge, 2004.

Gaynor, Mitchell L. *The Healing Power of Sound: Recovering from Life-Threatening Illness Using Sound, Voice, and Music.* Boston: Shambhala Publications, 1999.

Gernet, Jacques. *A History of Chinese Civilization.* Cambridge: Cambridge University Press, 1999.

Gikandi, Simon. "Editor's Column: This Thing Called Literature . . . What Work Does It Do?" *PMLA* 127, no. 1 (2012): 9–21.

_____. *The Routledge Encyclopedia of African Literature.* London: Routledge, 2009.

Gilbert, Erik T., and Jonathan T. Reynolds. *Africa in World History.* New York: Pearson, 2011.

Gilbert, Sandra, and Susan Gubar, ed. *Feminist Literary Theory and Criticism: A Norton Reader.* New York: W. W. Norton & Company, 2007.

_____. *Norton Anthology of Literature by Women.* New York: W. W. Norton & Company, 2007.

Giroux, Henry. *Border Crossings: Cultural Workers and the Politics of Education.* London: Routledge, 2005.

_____. "Cultural Studies, Public Pedagogy, and the Responsibility of Intellectuals." *Communication and Critical/Cultural Studies* 1, no. 1 (2004).

_____. *Education and the Crisis of Public Values.* New York: Peter Lang, 2011.

_____. *Zombie Politics and Culture in the Age of Casino Capitalism.* New York: Peter Lang, 2010.

Gless, Darryl, and Barbara Herrnstein Smith, ed. *The Politics of Liberal Education.* Durham: Duke University Press, 1991.

Glyer, Diana, and David L. Weeks, ed. *The Liberal Arts in Higher Education: Challenging Assumptions, Exploring Possibilities.* Lanham: University Press of America, 1998.

Godden, Richard. "Labor, Language, and Finance Capital." *PMLA* 126, no. 2 (2011): 412–21.

Gombrich, Ernst Hans. *The Story of Art.* London: Phaidon Press, 1995.

Gowdy, John, and Jon D. Erickson. "The Approach of Ecological Economics." *Cambridge Journal of Economics* (2005): 207–22.

Graff, Gerald. *Beyond the Culture Wars: How Teaching the Conflicts Can Revitalize American Education.* New York: W. W. Norton & Company, 1993.

Graham-Dixon, Andrew. *Art: Over 2,500 Works from Cave to Contemporary.* New York: DK Publishing, 2008.

Gray, Hannah. *Searching for Utopia: Universities and Their Histories.* Berkeley: University of California Press, 2012.

Greenwald, Michael L., Roberto Dario Pomo, and Roger Schultz, ed. *The Longman Anthology of Drama and Theater: A Global Perspective.* London: Longman, 2001.

Grewal, Inderpal, and Caren Kaplan. *An Introduction to Women's Studies: Gender in a Transnational World*. New York: McGraw-Hill, 2005.

Grote, John E. *Paideia Agonistes: The Lost Soul of Modern Education*. Lanham, MD: University Press of America, 2000.

Guillory, John. *Cultural Capital*. Chicago: University of Chicago Press, 1993.

Gutek, Gerald L. *New Perspectives on Philosophy and Education*. Columbus: Pearson, 2008.

Habermas, Jürgen. *The Philosophical Discourse of Modernity*. Cambridge, MA: MIT Press, 1987.

Hall, Donald E. *Queer Theories*. Basingstoke: Palgrave, 2003.

Haraway, Donna. *Simians, Cyborgs, and Women*. New York: Routledge, 1991.

Harpham, Geoffrey Galt. *The Humanities and the Dream of America*. Chicago: University of Chicago Press, 2011.

_____. "The Humanities Value." *Chronicle of Higher Education*, March 2009.

Harris, Julian, ed. *The Humanities: An Appraisal*. Madison: The University of Wisconsin Press, 1962.

Hausman, Daniel M., and Michael S. McPherson. *Economic Analysis and Moral Philosophy*. Cambridge: Cambridge University Press, 1996.

Havel, Vaclav. *The Art of the Impossible: Politics as Morality in Practice*. Translated by Paul Anson. New York: Knopf, 1997.

Hawking, Stephen. *A Brief History of Time*. New York: Bantam Books, 1988.

_____. *The Grand Design*. New York: Bantam Books, 2010.

Hayles, N. Katherine. *How We Became Posthuman: Virtual Bodies in Cybernetics, Literature, and Informatics*. Chicago: University of Chicago Press, 1999.

Heidegger, Martin. *Basic Writings*. Edited by Farrell Krell. New York: Harper Perennial, 2008.

_____. *Parmenides*. Translated by André Schuwer and Richard Rojcewicz. Bloomington: Indiana University Press, 1998.

_____. *The Question Concerning Technology and Other Essays*. Translated and with an Introduction by William Lovitt. New York: Harper Torchbooks, 1982.

Herman, David, James Phelan, Peter J. Rabinowitz, Brian Richardson, and Robyn Warhol, ed. *Narrative Theory: Core Concepts and Critical Debates*. Columbus: Ohio State University Press, 2012.

Hernández, Adriana. *Pedagogy, Democracy, and Feminism: Rethinking the Public Sphere*. Stony Brook: State University of New York Press, 1997.

Hinton, David, ed. *Classical Chinese Poetry: An Anthology*. New York: Farrar, Straus and Giroux, 2010.

Hirsch, David. *The Deconstruction of Literature: Criticism after Auschwitz*. Hanover: Brown University Press, 1991.

Hirsch, Eric Donald. *Cultural Literacy: What Every American Needs to Know*. New York: Vintage Books, 1988.

_____. *The Knowledge Deficit. Closing the Shocking Education Gap for American Children*. New York: Houghton Mifflin, 2007.

Hirsch, Marianne. *The Generation of Postmemory: Writing and Visual Culture After the Holocaust*. New York: Columbia University Press, 2012.

Holton, Gerald, ed. *Science and Culture: A Study of Cohesive and Disjunctive Forces*. Boston: Houghton Mifflin, 1965.

Homer. *The Odyssey*. Translated by Robert Fagles. Introduction and Notes by Bernard Knox. New York: Penguin Classics, 1997.

hooks, bell. *Teaching Community: A Pedagogy of Hope*. New York: Routledge, 2007.

_____. *Teaching to Transgress: Education as the Practice of Freedom*. New York: Routledge, 1994.

_____. *Teaching Critical Thinking: Practical Wisdom*. New York: Routledge, 2010.

Horkheimer, Max, and Theodor Adorno. *Dialectic of Enlightenment*. Stanford, CA: Stanford University Press, 2002.

Huesemann, Michael, and Joyce Huesemann. *Techno-Fix: Why Technology Won't Save Us or the Environment*. Gabriola Island, BC: New Society Publishers, 2011.

Hugo, Victor. *William Shakespeare*. Freeport: Books for Libraries Press, 1970.

Hunter, James Davison. *Culture Wars: The Struggle to Define America.* New York: Basic Books, 1992.

Husserl, Edmund. *The Crisis of European Sciences and Transcendental Phenomenology.* Translated by David Carr. Evanston, IL: Northwestern University Press, 1970.

Hutcheon, Linda. *The Politics of Postmodernism.* London: Routledge, 2002.

Huxley, Thomas Henry. *Science and Culture and Other Essays.* Boston: Adamant Media Corporation, 2005.

Ingersoll, Richard, and Spiro Kostof. *World Architecture: A Cross-Cultural History.* Oxford: Oxford University Press, 2012.

Irigaray, Luce. *Speculum of the Other Woman.* Translated by Gillian C. Gill. Ithaca, NY: Cornell University Press, 1985.

Jacoby, Russell. *The Last Intellectuals: American Culture in the Age of Academe.* New York: Basic Books, Inc., 2000.

Jagose, Annamarie. *Queer Theory: An Introduction.* New York: New York University Press, 1997.

Jameson, Fredric. *Archaeologies of the Future: The Desired Called Utopia and Other Science Fictions.* London: Verso, 2005.

————. *The Political Unconscious: Narrative as a Socially Symbolic Act.* Ithaca, NY: Cornell University Press, 1981.

————. *Postmodernism, or, the Cultural Logic of Late Capitalism.* Durham, NC: Duke University Press, 1991.

Jan van Gelder, Geert, ed. *Classical Arabic Literature: A Library of Arabic Literature Anthology.* New York: New York University Press, 2013.

Janicaud, Dominique. *On the Human Condition.* Translated by Eileen Brennan. London: Routledge, 2005.

Jauss, Hans Robert. *Toward an Aesthetic of Reception.* Translated by Timothy Bahti. Brighton: Harvester Press, 1982.

Jay, Paul. *The Humanities "Crisis" and the Future of Literary Studies.* New York: Palgrave Macmillan, 2014.

Jayyusi, Salma Khadra. *Short Arab Plays: An Anthology.* New York: Interlink Books, 2003.

Jonas, Hans. *The Imperative of Responsibility: In Search of an Ethics for the Technological Age.* Chicago: The University of Chicago Press, 1985.

Jones, Amelia. *Seeing Differently: A History and Theory Identification and the Visual Arts.* New York: Routledge, 2012.

Jorgensen, Estelle. *Transforming Music Education.* Indianapolis: Indiana University Press, 2008.

Kamenetz, Anya. *DIY U: Edupunks, Edupreneurs, and the Coming Transformation of Higher Education.* New York: Chelsea Green Publishing, 2010.

Kang, Kyung-Sook. *Korean Ceramics.* Washington, DC: The Korean Foundation, 2013.

Kant, Immanuel. *Critique of Pure Reason.* Translated, edited, and with an introduction by Marcus Weigelt. New York: Penguin Classics, 2008.

Kaplan, David M., ed. *Readings in the Philosophy of Technology.* Lanham, MD: Rowman & Littlefield Publishers, 2004.

Kaplan, E. Ann. *The Politics of Research.* New Brunswick, NJ: Rutgers University Press, 1997.

Kaufmann, Walter. *The Future of the Humanities.* London: Transaction Publishers, 1995.

Keen, Suzanne. *Empathy and the Novel.* Oxford: Oxford University Press, 2010.

Keene, Donald. *Anthology of Japanese Literature: From the Earliest Era to the Mid-Nineteenth Century.* New York: Grove Books, 1994.

Kemp, Sandra, ed. *Feminisms.* Oxford: Oxford University Press, 1997.

Kernan, Elvin, ed. *What's Happened to the Humanities?* Princeton, NJ: Princeton University Press, 1997.

Kerr, Clark. *The Uses of the University.* Cambridge, MA: Harvard University Press, 2001.

Keynes, John Maynard. *The General Theory of Employment, Interest, and Money.* Cambridge: MacMillan, 1936.

King, Martin Luther Jr. *The Essential Writings and Speeches of Martin Luther King, Jr.* Edited by James M. Washington. New York: HarperCollins Publishers, 1991.

————. *Letter from the Birmingham Jail.* New York: Harper Collins, 1994.

————. "The Purpose of Education." *The Maroon Tiger*, 1947.

Klein, Richard. "The Future of Literary Criticism." *PMLA* 125, no. 4 (2010): 920–23.

Kleiner, Fred S. *Gardner's Art through the Ages: A Global History.* Independence, KY: Cengage Learning, 2008.

Knapp, Steven. "The Enduring Dilemma of the Humanities." *The Phi Beta Kappa Society*, March 2011.

Knowles, David, ed. *The Evolution of Medieval Thought.* Ed. D. E. Luscombe and C. N. L. Brooke. London: Longman Group Limited, 1988.

Koyré, Alexandre. *From the Closed World to the Infinite Universe.* Baltimore: The Johns Hopkins University Press, 1957.

Kramer, Lawrence. *Why Classical Music Still Matters.* Berkeley: University of California Press, 2009.

Kristiansen, Staale Johannes, and Svein Rise. *Key Theological Thinkers: From Modern to Postmodern.* Burlington: Ashgate Publishing, 2013.

Kronman, Anthony T. *Education's End: Why Our Colleges and Universities Have Given Up on the Meaning of Life.* New Haven: Yale University Press, 2007.

Kuhn, Thomas S. *The Structures of Scientific Revolutions: 50 th Anniversary Edition.* Chicago: University of Chicago Press, 2012.

LaCapra, Dominick. *History in Transit: Experience, Identity, Critical Theory.* Ithaca, NY: Cornell University Press, 2004.

Laclau, Ernesto. "Politics and the Limits of Modernity." In *Universal Abandon?: The Politics of Postmodernism*, edited by Andrew Ross. Minneapolis: University of Minnesota Press, 1988.

————. *The Rhetorical Foundations of Society.* New York: Verso, 2014.

Lacoue-Labarthe, Philippe. *Poetry as Experience.* Translated by Andrea Tarnowski. Stanford, CA: Stanford University Press, 1999.

Landy, Joshua. *How to Do Things with Fiction.* Oxford: Oxford University Press, 2012.

Lane, Richard J. *Global Literary Theory: An Anthology.* New York: Routledge, 2013.

Lang, Kevin. *Poverty and Discrimination.* Princeton, NJ: Princeton University Press, 2007.

Langer, Lawrence L., ed. *Art from the Ashes: A Holocaust Anthology.* New York: Oxford University Press, 1995.

Latour, Bruno. *Politics of Nature: How to Bring the Sciences into Democracy.* Translated by Catherine Porter. Cambridge, MA: Harvard University Press, 2004.

Lawall, Sarah, ed. *The Norton Anthology of Western Literature: Vols. 1–2.* New York: W. W. Norton & Company, 2006.

Lawall, Sarah, Maynard Mack, Jerome W. Clinton, and Robert Lyons, ed. *The Norton Anthology of World Literature: Beginnings to 1650.* New York: W. W. Norton & Company, 2003.

————. *The Norton Anthology of World Literature: 1650 to the Present.* New York: W. W. Norton & Company, 2003.

Lawler, James R. *The Language of French Symbolism.* Princeton, NJ: Princeton University Press, 1969.

————, ed. *Paul Valéry: An Anthology.* Princeton, NJ: Princeton University Press, 1977.

Leach, Jim. "Defending the Liberal Arts." *American Council of Learned Societies.* Washington DC, May 2011.

————. "Humanities and Citizenship." *National Academy of Education 2011 Annual Meeting.* George Washington University, October 2011.

————. "STEM and the Humanities." *Graduate College Distinguished Lecture*, University of Illinois, Urbana-Champaign, April 2013.

Lechuga, Vincente M. *The Changing Landscape of the Academic Profession.* New York: Routledge, 2006.

Ledwith, Sara, and Antonella Ciancio. "Crisis Forces 'Dismal Science' to Get Real." *Reuters*, July 2012.

Leeman, Richard W., and Bernard K. Duffy, ed. *The Will of a People: A Critical Anthology of Great African American Speeches.* Carbondale: Southern Illinois University Press, 2012.

Leeming, David Adams, ed. *The World of Myth: An Anthology.* Oxford: Oxford University Press, 1992.

Leitch, Vincent B., ed. *The Norton Anthology of Theory and Criticism.* New York: W. W. Norton & Company, 2010.

Lepage, Peter G., Carolyn Martin, and Mohsen Mostafavi, ed. *Do the Humanities Have to Be Useful?* Ithaca, NY: Cornell University Press, 2006.

Levi, Albert W. *The Humanities Today.* Bloomington: Indiana University Press, 1970.

Levi, Primo. *Survival in Auschwitz.* Translated by Stuart Woolf. New York: First Touchtone Edition, 1996.

Levin, Amy, and Phoebe Stein Davis. "'Good Readers Make Good Doctors': Community Readings and the Health of the Community." *PMLA* 125, no. 2 (2010): 426–36.

Levinas, Emmanuel. *Entre Nous: On Thinking of the Other.* Translated by Michael B. Smith and Barbara Harshav. New York: Colombia University Press, 1998.

———. *Ethics and Infinity.* Conversations with Philippe Nemo. Translated by Richard A. Cohen. Pittsburgh: Duquesne University Press, 1985.

———. *Humanism of the Other.* Translated by Nidra Poller. Chicago: University of Illinois Press, 2005.

Levine, Caroline. *Provoking Democracy: Why We Need the Arts.* Malden, MA: Blackwell Publishing, 2007.

Levine, Peter. *The Future of Democracy: Developing the Next Generation of American Citizens.* Lebanon, NH: Tufts University Press, 2007.

Levine, Robert M., and John Crocitti. *The Brazil Reader: History, Culture, Politics.* Durham, NC: Duke University Press, 1999.

Levy, Daniel, and Natan Sznaider. *The Holocaust and Memory in the Global Age.* Translated by A. Oksiloff. Philadelphia: Temple University Press, 2006.

Lewin, D., A. Guilherme, and M. White, ed. *New Perspectives in Philosophy of Education: Ethics, Politics, and Religion.* London: Bloomsbury, 2014.

Lewis, Reina, and Sara Mills, ed. *Feminist Postcolonial Theory: A Reader.* New York: Routledge, 2003.

Lionnet, Françoise, ed. *Postcolonial Subjects: Francophone Women Authors.* Minneapolis: University of Minnesota Press, 1996.

Locke, John. *An Essay Concerning Human Understanding.* New York: Penguin Classics, 1997.

———. *Some Thoughts Concerning Education.* Mineola, NY: Dover Philosophical Classic, 2007.

———. *Two Treatises of Government.* New York: Merchant Books, 2011.

Luckhurst, Roger. *The Trauma Question.* London: Routledge, 2008.

Lutz, Mark A. *Economics for the Common Good.* New York: Routledge, 1999.

Lyotard, Jean-François. *Libidinal Economy.* Translated by Iain Hamilton Grant. Bloomington: Indiana University Press, 1993.

———. *Political Writings.* Translated by Bill Readings and Kevin Paul Geiman. Minneapolis: The University of Minnesota Press, 1993.

———. *The Postmodern Condition: A Report on Knowledge.* Translated by Geoff Bennington and Brian Massumi. Minneapolis: University of Minnesota Press, 1984.

Machiavelli, Niccolò. *The Prince.* Translated by Peter Bondanella. New York: Oxford University Press, 2008.

Mack, Maynard, Ed. *The Norton Anthology of World Masterpieces.* New York: W. W. Norton & Company, 1997.

Macrine, Sheila L., ed. *Critical Pedagogy in Uncertain Times: Hope and Possibilities.* New York: Palgrave, 2009.

Malraux, André. *The Voices of Silence.* Translated by Stuart Gilbert. Princeton, NJ: Princeton University Press, 1978.

Martenson, Chris. *The Crash Course: The Unsustainable Future of our Economy, Energy, and Environment.* Hoboken, NJ: John Wiley and Sons, 2011.

Martin, David F., and Lee Jacobus. *The Humanities through the Arts.* New York: McGraw-Hill, 2011.

Marx, Karl. *Selected Writings.* Edited by David McLellan. Oxford: Oxford University Press, 2000.

Marx, Karl, and Friedrich Engels. *The Communist Manifesto.* New York: Swenson & Kemp, 2013.

Maxwell, David W. "A Methodological Hypothesis for the Plight of the Humanities." *Bulletin of the American Association of University Professors* 54 (Spring 1968).

McCann, Carole, and Kim Seung-Kyung, ed. *Feminist Theory Reader: Local and Global Perspectives.* New York: Routledge, 2013.

McCloskey, Deirdre. *Knowledge and Persuasion in Economics.* Cambridge: Cambridge University Press, 1994.

_____. *The Rhetoric of Economics.* Madison: University of Wisconsin Press, 1983.

McRuer, Robert, and Michael F. Bérubé. *Crip Theory: Cultural Signs of Queerness and Disability.* New York: New York University Press, 2006.

Meadows, Donella H., Jorgen Randers, and Dennis L. Meadows. Limits to Growth: The 30-Year Update. Burlington, VT: Chelsea Green Publishing, 2004.

Mehta, Ved. *Portrait of India.* New Haven, CT: Yale University Press, 1993.

Menand, Louis. *The Future of Academic Freedom.* Chicago: Chicago University Press, 1998.

_____. "Live and Learn: Why We Have College." *The New Yorker*, June 6, 2011.

_____. The Marketplace of Ideas: Reform and Resistance in the American University. New York: W. W. Norton. 2010.

Mexal, Stephen J. "The Unintended Value of the Humanities." *The Chronicle Review*, 2010.

Meyer, Marvin, ed. *Reverence for Life: The Ethics of Albert Schweitzer for the Twenty-First Century.* Syracuse, NY: Syracuse University Press, 2002.

Mill, John Stuart. *Essays on Some Unsettled Questions of Political Economy.* Kitchener: Batoche Books, 2000.

_____. *On Liberty.* New York: Dover Publications, 2002.

Miller, Arthur J. *Einstein, Picasso: Space, Time, and the Beauty That Causes Havoc.* New York: Basic Books, 2002.

Miller, Richard E., and Kurt Spellmeyer. *The New Humanities Reader.* New York: Houghton Mifflin Company, 2006.

Miller, Toby. *Blow Up the Humanities.* Philadelphia: Temple University Press, 2012.

Mirowski, Philip. *More Heat Than Light: Economics as Social Physics, Physics as Nature's Economics.* New York: Cambridge University Press, 1989.

_____. *Never Let a Serious Crisis Go to Waste: How Neoliberalism Survived the Financial Meltdown.* New York: Verso, 2014.

Mitchell, David T., and Sharon Snyder. *Narrative Prosthesis: Disability and the Dependencies of Discourse.* Ann Arbor: University of Michigan Press, 2001.

Moi, Toril. *Sexual/Textual Politics: Feminist Literary Theory.* New York: Routledge, 2002.

Montaigne, Michel de. *The Complete Essays of Montaigne.* Translated by Donald M. Frame. Stanford: Stanford University Press, 1976.

Montesquieu, Charles Louis de Secondat. *Persian Letters.* Translated by C. J. Betts. New York: Penguin Classics, 1973.

_____. *The Spirit of Laws.* Translated by Thomas Nugent. New York: Cosimo Classics, 2011.

Morin, Edgar, and Pietro Corsi. *Seven Complex Lessons in Education for the Future.* Paris: Unesco Publishing, 2003.

Morrison, Toni, Gayatri Chakravorty Spivak, and Ngahuia Te Awekotuku. "Guest Column: Roundtable on the Future of the Humanities in a Fragmented World." *PMLA* 120, no. 3 (2005): 715–23.

Mulcahy, Donal G. *The Educated Person: Toward a New Paradigm for Liberal Education.* Lanham, MD: Rowman & Littlefield Publishers, 2008.

Murdoch, Iris. *The Sovereignty of the Good.* New York: Routledge, 2001.

Murray, Chris, ed. *Key Writers on Art: The Twentieth-Century.* New York: Routledge, 2003.

Nafisi, Azar. *Reading Lolita in Teheran: A Memoir in Books.* New York: Random House, 2003.

Nelson, Julie A. *Economics for Humans.* Chicago: University of Chicago Press, 2006.

Newman, John Henry. *The Idea of a University.* Frank M. Turner, ed. New Haven, CT: Yale University Press, 1996.

Nietzsche, Friedrich. *Beyond Good and Evil.* Translated by Walter Kaufmann. New York: Vintage Books Edition, 1989.

_____. *The Birth of Tragedy: Out of the Spirit of Music.* Translated by Shaun Whiteside. New York: Penguin, 1994.

_____. *Ecce Homo: How One Becomes What One Is.* Translated by Thomas Wayne. New York: Algora Publishing, 2004.

Nixon, Jon. *Higher Education and the Public Good: Imagining the University.* London: Bloomsbury, 2011.

_____. *Interpretive Pedagogies for Higher Education: Arendt, Berger, Said, Nussbaum, and Their Legacies.* London: Bloomsbury, 2012.

Noddings, Nel. *Critical Lessons: What Our Schools Should Teach.* New York: Cambridge University Press, 2006.

_____. *Educating Moral People: A Caring Alternative to Character Education.* New York: Teachers College Press, 2002.

_____. *Philosophy of Education.* Boulder, CO: Westview Press, 2012.

Norris, Christopher. *What's Wrong with Postmodernism?: Critical Theory and the Ends of Philosophy.* Baltimore: Johns Hopkins University Press, 1990.

Nussbaum, Martha. *Cultivating Humanity.* Cambridge, MA: Harvard University Press, 1998.

_____. *Love's Knowledge: Essays on Philosophy and Literature.* New York: Oxford University Press, 1992.

_____. *Not for Profit: Why Democracy Needs the Humanities.* Princeton, NJ: Princeton University Press, 2010.

_____. *Poetic Justice. The Literary Imagination and Public Life.* Boston: Beacon Press, 1997.

Nye, Joseph S. *The Paradox of American Power.* New York: Oxford University Press, 2002.

Okasha, Samir. *Philosophy of Science: A Very Short Introduction.* Oxford: Oxford University Press, 2002.

Olson, Gary A., and John W. Presley. *The Future of Higher Education: Perspectives from America's Academic Leaders.* New York: Paradigm Publishers, 2010.

Ornstein, Allan C., and Daniel U. Levine. *Foundations of Education.* New York: Houghton Mifflin Company, 2003.

Ortega y Gasset, José. *Mission of the University.* With an Introduction by Clark Kerr. New York: Transactions, 1991.

Palmer, Joy A., ed. *Fifty Major Thinkers on Education: From Confucius to Dewey.* London: Routledge, 2001.

_____. *Fifty Modern Thinkers on Education: From Piaget to the Present.* London: Routledge, 2001.

Paxson, Christina H. "The Economic Case for Saving the Humanities." *New Republic*, August 2013.

Payne, Michael, and John Schad, ed. *Life after Theory: Interviews with Jacques Derrida, Sir Frank Kermode, Toril Moi, and Christopher Norris.* London: Continuum, 2004.

Perry, Lewis. *Civil Disobedience: An American Tradition.* New Haven: Yale University Press, 2013.

Peters, Michael, A. and Gert Biesta. *Derrida, Deconstruction, and the Politics of Pedagogy.* New York: Peter Lang, 2009.

Peterson, Michael, William Hasker, Bruce Reichenbach, and David Basinger, ed. *Philosophy of Religion: Selected Reading.* Oxford: Oxford University Press, 2001.

Peyer, Bernd C., ed. *American Indian Nonfiction: An Anthology of Writings, 1760s–1930s.* Norman: University of Oklahoma Press, 2007.

Peyre, Henri. *Observations on Life, Literature, and Learning in America.* Carbondale: Southern Illinois University Press, 1961.

Phelan, James, and Peter J. Rabinowitz, ed. *A Companion to Narrative Theory.* Oxford: Blackwell Publishing, 2008.

Pico della Mirandola, Giovanni. *Oration on the Dignity of Man.* Edited by Francesco Borghesi, Michael Papio, and Massimo Riva. New York: Cambridge University Press, 2012.

Piketty, Thomas. *Capital in the Twenty-First Century.* Translated by Arthur Goldhammer. New York: Belknap Press, 2014.

Plato. *Protagoras.* Translated by C. C. W. Taylor. New York: Oxford University Press, 2009.

————. *The Republic.* Translated by Desmond Lee. New York: Penguin Classic, 2007.

Polanyi, Michael, and Harry Prosch. *Meaning.* Chicago: University of Chicago Press, 1975.

Post, Jennifer C. *Ethnomusicology: A Contemporary Reader.* New York: Routledge, 2010.

Postman, Neil. *Building a Bridge to the 18th Century.* New York: Vintage Books, 1999.

————. *The End of Education: Redefining the Value of School.* New York: Vintage, 1996.

Preziosi, Donald, ed. *The Art of Art History: A Critical Anthology.* Oxford: Oxford University Press, 2009.

Proust, Marcel. *In Search of Lost Time.* Translated by C. K. Scott Moncrieff and Terence Kilmartin. New York: Modern Library, 2003.

————. "On Reading." *Marcel Proust and John Ruskin on Reading.* Foreword by Eric Karpeles. London: Hesperus Press, 2011.

Puar, Jasbir K., and Julie Livingston. *Social Text: Interspecies.* Durham, NC: Duke University Press, 2011.

Puchner, Martin, ed. *The Norton Anthology of World Literature.* New York: W. W. Norton & Company, 2012.

Rabelais, François. *Gargantua and Pantagruel.* Translated by M. A. Screech. New York: Penguin Classics, 2006.

Rancière, Jacques. *The Ignorant Schoolmaster: Five Lessons in Intellectual Emancipation.* Translated with an introduction by Kristin Ross. Stanford, CA: Stanford University Press, 1991.

————. *The Politics of Aesthetics: The Distribution of the Sensible.* Translated by Gabriel Rockhill. New York: Continuum, 2004.

Rawls, John. *A Theory of Justice.* New York: Belknap Press, 2005.

Readings, Bill. *The University in Ruins.* Cambridge, MA: Harvard University Press, 1997.

Reimer, Bennett. *A Philosophy of Music Education.* New York: Prentice Hall, 2003.

Reinvigorating the Humanities: Enhancing Research and Education on Campus and Beyond. Association of American Universities, 2004.

Report of the Commission on the Humanities. New York: American Council of Learned Societies, 1964.

Report of the Commission on the Humanities and Social Sciences: The Heart of the Matter: The Humanities and Social Sciences. Cambridge: American Academy of Arts & Sciences, 2013.

Report of the Commission on the Humanities Sponsored by the Rockefeller Foundation: The Humanities in American Life. Berkeley: University of California Press, 1980.

Report of the Task Force on General Education. Harvard University Faculty of Arts and Sciences. Cambridge, MA: Harvard College, 2007.

Reynolds, John Mark. *The Great Books Reader.* Minneapolis, MN: Bethany House Publishers, 2011.

Rice, Alan. *Radical Narratives of the Black Atlantic.* New York: Continuum, 2002.

Rich, Adrienne. *On Lies, Secrets and Silence.* New York: W. W. Norton and Company, 1979.

Ricoeur, Paul. *Memory, History, Forgetting.* Translated by Kathleen Blamey and David Pellauer. Chicago: University of Chicago Press, 2006.

Ridder-Symoens, Hilde de, ed. *A History of the University in Europe. Vol. I: Universities in the Middle Ages.* Cambridge University Press, 1992.

Rink, John, ed. *The Practice of Performance: Studies in Musical Interpretation.* Cambridge: Cambridge University Press, 2005.

Roche, Mark. *Why Choose the Liberal Arts?* Notre Dame: University of Notre Dame Press, 2010.

————. *Why Literature Matters in the 21st Century.* New Haven, CT: Yale University Press, 2004.

Rooney, Thomas. *Humanities: A Case Study.* Washington, DC: National Education Association, 1989.

Rorty, Richard. *Achieving Our Country: Leftist Thought in Twentieth-Century America.* Cambridge, MA: Harvard University Press, 1998.
_____. *Contingency, Irony, and Solidarity.* Cambridge: Cambridge University Press, 1989.
_____. *Truth and Progress.* Cambridge: Cambridge University Press, 1998.
Rosen, Charles. *Freedom and the Arts: Essays on Music and Literature.* Cambridge: Harvard University Press, 2012.
Rosenberg, Alex. *The Atheist's Guide to Reality: Enjoying Life without Illusions.* New York: W. W. Norton and Company, 2012.
_____. *Philosophy of Science.* London: Routledge, 2000.
Rosenberg, Donna. *World Mythology: An Anthology of the Great Myths and Epics.* New York: McGraw-Hill, 2001.
Roskies, David G., and Naomi Diamant. *Holocaust Literature: A History and Guide.* Waltham, MA: Brandeis University Press, 2012.
Roth, Klas, and Ilan Gur-Ze'ev, eds. *Education in the Era of Globalization.* Dordrecht: Springer, 2007.
Rothberg, Michael. *Multidirectional Memory: Remembering the Holocaust in the Age of Decolonization.* Stanford, CA: Stanford University Press, 2009.
Rousseau, Jean-Jacques. *Emile, or on Education.* Introduction, Translation, and Notes by Allan Bloom. New York: Basic Books, 1979.
Rowe, William, L. *The Philosophy of Religion: An Introduction.* Independence, KY: Cengage Learning, 2006.
Ruark, Jennifer. "Defenders of the Humanities Look for New Ways to Explain Their Value." *Chronicle of Higher Education Commentary*, 2011.
Rudolph, Frederick, ed. *Essays on Education in the Early Republic.* Cambridge, MA: Harvard University Press, 1965.
Russo, John Paul. *The Future without a Past. The Humanities in a Technological Society.* Columbia: University of Missouri Press, 2005.
Saad-Filho, Alfredo, and Deborah Johnson, eds. *Neoliberalism: A Critical Reader.* London: Pluto Press, 2005.
Sacks, Oliver. *Musicophilia: Tales of Music and the Brain.* New York: Vintage, 2008.
Said, Edward W. *Humanism and Democratic Criticism.* New York: Columbia University Press, 2004.
_____. *Orientalism.* New York: Pantheon Books, 1978.
_____. *Reflections on Exile.* Cambridge, MA: Harvard University Press, 2000.
_____. *The World, the Text and the Critic.* Cambridge, MA: Harvard University Press, 1983.
Saint Augustine. *Confessions.* Translated by Henry Chadwick. Oxford: Oxford University Press, 2009.
Sandel, Michael J. *Justice: What's the Right Thing to Do?* New York: Farrar, Straus and Giroux, 2010.
_____. *What Money Can't Buy: The Moral Limits of Markets.* New York: Farrar, Straus and Giroux, 2012.
Sarkhosh Curtis, Vesta, and Sheila R. Canby. *Persian Love Poetry.* London: British Museum Press, 2013.
Sartre, Jean-Paul. *What Is Literature?* Translated by Bernard Frechtman. London: Routledge Classics, 2001.
Sayre, Henry M. *Discovering the Humanities.* New York: Prentice Hall, 2010.
_____. *The Humanities: Culture, Continuity, and Change.* New York: Pearson, 2011.
Schlefer, Jonathan. *The Assumptions Economists Make.* New York: Belknap Press, 2012.
Schleifer, Ronald, and Jerry B. Vannatta. *The Chief Concern of Medicine: The Integration of the Medical Humanities and Narrative Knowledge into Medical Practices.* Ann Arbor: University of Michigan Press, 2013.
Scholes, Robert. "Presidential Address 2004: The Humanities in a Posthumanist World." *PMLA* 120, no. 3 (2005): 724–33.
Schumacher, Ernst Friedrich. *Small Is Beautiful. Economics as If People Mattered.* New York: Harper Perennial, 2010.
Schumpeter, Joseph A. *History of Economic Analysis.* Oxford: Oxford University Press, 1996.

Schwartz, Regina. *Transcendence: Philosophy, Literature, and Theology Approach the Beyond.* London: Routledge, 2004.

Schwarz, Daniel R. *The Case for a Humanistic Poetics.* Philadelphia: University of Pennsylvania Press, 1991.

Sen, Amartya. *Development as Freedom.* New York: Alfred A. Knopf, 2001.

———. *The Idea of Justice.* Cambridge, MA: Harvard University Press, 2011.

———. *On Ethics and Economics.* Malden, MA: Blackwell Publishing, 1987.

———. *Poverty and Famines: An Essay on Entitlement and Deprivation.* Oxford: Oxford University Press, 1983.

Seneca, Lucius Annaeus. *Ad Lucilium Epistulae Morales.* Translated by Richard M. Gummere. Cambridge: Harvard University Press, 1967.

Shapin, Steven. *The Scientific Revolution.* Chicago: University of Chicago Press, 1998.

Shelley, Percy Bysshe. *Political Writings including A Defense of Poetry.* New York, Appleton-Century-Crofts, 1970.

Shils, Edward. *The Calling of Education: The "Academic Ethic" and Other Essays on Higher Education.* Edited by Steven Grosby. Chicago: University of Chicago Press, 1997.

Shiva, Vendana. *Making Peace with the Earth.* London: Pluto Press, 2013.

———. *Monocultures of the Mind: Perspectives on Biodiversity and Biotechnology.* London: Zed Books, 1993.

Siebers, Tobin Anthony. *Disability Theory (Corporealities: Discourses of Disability).* Ann Arbor: University of Michigan Press, 2008.

Singer, Peter, and Renata Singer, ed. *The Moral of the Story: An Anthology of Ethics through Literature.* Malden, MA: Blackwell Publishing, 2005.

Skorton, David. "State of the University Address." Cornell University, 2010.

Slouka, Mark. "Dehumanized: When Math and Science Rule the School." *Harper's Magazine,* 2009.

Small, Helen H. *The Value of the Humanities.* New York: Oxford University Press, 2013.

Smeyers, Paul, Richard Smith, and Paul Standish. *The Therapy of Education: Philosophy, Happiness and Personal Growth.* New York: Palgrave Macmillan, 2007.

Smith, Adam. *The Theory of Moral Sentiments.* New York: Empire Books, 2013.

———. *The Wealth of Nations.* New York: Bantham Classics, 2003.

Snow, Charles Percy. *The Two Cultures and the Scientific Revolution.* Eastford, CT: Martino Fine Books, 2013.

Snyder, Sharon L., and David T. Mitchell. *Cultural Locations of Disability.* Chicago: University of Chicago Press, 2006.

Soeiro, Ricardo Gil, and Sofia Tavares, ed. *Rethinking the Humanities: Paths and Challenges.* Cambridge: Cambridge Scholars Publishing, 2012.

Solomon, Robert C., and Kathleen M. Higgins, ed. *From Africa to Zen: An Invitation to World Philosophy.* Lanham, MD: Rowman & Littlefield Publishers, 2003.

Solzhenitsyn, Aleksandr. *The Gulag Archipelago: An Experiment in Literary Investigation.* Translated by Thomas P. Whitney. New York: Harper Perennial, 2007.

Sontag, Susan. *On Photography.* New York: Picador, 2001.

Spellmeyer, Kurt. *Reinventing the Humanities for the Twenty-First Century.* Albany: State University of New York Press, 2003.

Spinoza, Benedict de. *Ethics.* Translated by Edwin Curley. New York: Penguin Classics, 2005.

Spivak, Gayatri Chakravorty. *An Aesthetic Education in the Era of Globalization.* Cambridge: Harvard University Press, 2013.

———. *Death of a Discipline.* New York: Columbia University Press, 2003.

———. *In Other Worlds: Essays in Cultural Politics.* London: Routledge, 2006.

State Humanities Councils. *A Brief History and Overview.* Arlington: Federation of State Humanities Councils, 2004.

Stavans, Llan. *The Norton Anthology of Latino Literature.* New York: W. W. Norton & Company, 2011.

Stavins, Robert N. *Economics of the Environment: Selected Readings.* New York: W. W. Norton & Company, 2012.

Steinbeck, John. *The Grapes of Wrath.* New York: Alfred A. Knopf, 1993.

Steinberg, Michael. *Choral Masterworks: A Listener's Guide.* Oxford: Oxford University Press, 2005.

———. *The Symphony: A Listener's Guide.* Oxford: Oxford University Press, 1998.

Steiner, Georges. "The Muses' Farewell." *Salmagundi* 135–36 (2002): 148–56.

Stern, David, ed. *The Anthology in Jewish Literature.* New York: Oxford University Press, 2004.

Stierlin, Henri. *Persian Art and Architecture.* London: Tames & Hudson, 2012.

Stiglitz, Joseph. *Globalization and Its Discontents.* New York: W. W. Norton & Company, 2003.

———. *The Great Divide: Unequal Societies and What We Can Do About Them.* New York: W. W. Norton Company, 2015.

———. *The Price of Inequality: How Today's Divided Society Endangers Our Future.* New York: W. W. Norton Company, 2013.

Sturken, Marita, and Lisa Cartwright. *Practices of Looking: An Introduction to Visual Culture.* Oxford: Oxford University Press, 2009.

Sutter, Daniel, and Rex Pjesky. "Where Would Adam Smith Publish Today? The Near Absence of Math-Free Research in Top Journals." *Econ Journal Watch* 4, no. 2 (2007): 230–40.

Szarkowski, John. *The Photographer's Eye.* New York: The Museum of Modern Art, 2007.

Tadjo, Véronique. *The Shadow of Imana.* Translated by Véronique Wakerley. Oxford: Heinemann, 2002.

Taruskin, Richard, and Piero Weiss. *Music in the Western World: A History in Documents.* Independence, KY: Cengage Learning, 2007.

Taylor, Charles. *Sources of the Self: The Making of the Modern Identity.* Cambridge, MA: Harvard University Press, 1992.

Thomson Klein, Julie. *Humanities, Culture, and Interdisciplinarity: The Changing American Academy.* Stony Brook: State University of New York Press, 2005.

Tinker, Irene, ed. *Persistent Inequalities: Women and World Development.* New York: Oxford University Press, 1990.

Titon, Jeff Todd, ed. *Worlds of Music: An Introduction to the Music of the World's Peoples.* Independence: Cengage Learning, 2008.

Tocqueville, Alexis de. *Democracy in America.* Translated by Arthur Goldhammer. New York: The Library of America, 2004.

Todorov, Tzvetan. *Imperfect Garden: The Legacy of Humanism.* Translated by Carol Cosman. Princeton, NJ: Princeton University Press, 2002.

Tolstoy, Leo. *War and Peace.* Translated by Richard Pevear and Larissa Volokhonsky. New York: First Vintage Classics, 2007.

Totten, Samuel, and Paul R. Bartrop, Ed. *Dictionary of Genocide.* Westport, CT: Greenwood Press, 2008.

Trifonas, Peter Pericles, and Michael A. Peters, eds. *Deconstructing Derrida: Tasks for the New Humanities.* New York: Palgrave MacMillan, 2005.

Tuchman, Gaye. *Wannabe U: Inside the Corporate University.* Chicago: Chicago University Press, 2009.

Turkle, Sherry. "How Computers Change the Way We Think." *The Chronicle Review* 50, no. 21 (2004): B 26.

———. *Reclaiming Conversation: The Power of Talk in a Digital Age.* New York: Penguin Press, 2015.

Ulin, David L. *The Lost Art of Reading: Why Books Matter in a Distracted Time.* Seattle: Sasquatch Books, 2010.

Ungar, Sanford J. "7 Majors Misperceptions about the Liberal Arts." *Chronicle of Higher Education,* February 2010.

Van Voost, Robert E. *Anthology of World Scriptures.* Independence: Cengage Learning, 2013.

Vaughan-Lee, Llewellyn, ed. *Spiritual Ecology: The Cry of the Earth.* Point Reyes: The Golden Sufi Center, 2013.

Veninga, James F. *The Humanities and the Civic Imagination: Collected Addresses and Essays 1978–1998.* Denton: University of North Texas Press, 1999.

Viereck, George Sylvester. "What Life Means to Einstein." *Saturday Evening Post*, October 26, 1929.

Visona, Monica B., Robin Poynor, Herbert M. Cole, and Preston Biler. *A History of Art in Africa.* New York: Pearson, 2007.

Walker, Gordon. *Environmental Justice: Concepts, Evidence and Politics.* London: Routledge, 2012.

Walling, Donovan. *Under Construction: The Role of the Arts and Humanities in Postmodern Schooling.* Bloomington, IN: Phi Delta Kappa Educational Foundation, 1997.

Waring, Marilyn. *If Women Counted: A New Feminist Economics.* New York: Harper Collins, 1990.

Washington, James Melvin, ed. *A Testament of Hope: The Essential Writings of Martin Luther King Jr.* San Francisco: Harper, 1991.

Watson, Robert N. "The Humanities Really Do Produce a Profit." *Chronicle of Higher Education Commentary*, March 2010.

Weil, Simone. *Gravity and Grace.* Translated by Emma Crawford and Mario von der Ruhr. London: Routledge, 2002.

_____. *Waiting for God.* Translated by Emma Crawford. New York: Harper Perennial, 2009.

Weisbuch, Robert. "Six Proposals to Revive the Humanities." *Chronicle of Higher Education Commentary*, 1999.

West, Cornel. *Democracy Matters: Winning the Fight against Imperialism.* London: Penguin, 2004.

White, Lawrence H. *The Clash of Economic Ideas: The Great Policy Debates and Experiments of the Last Hundred Years.* Cambridge: Cambridge University Press, 2012.

Wiarda, Howard J. *The Soul of Latin America: The Cultural and Political Tradition.* New Haven, CT: Yale University Press, 2003.

Wiesel, Elie. *Night .* Translated by Marion Wiesel. New York: Hill and Wang, 2006.

Wilson, Edward O. *Consilience. The Unity of Knowledge.* New York: Alfred A. Knopf, 1998.

_____. *On Human Nature.* Cambridge, MA: Harvard University Press, 2004.

Wolfe, Cary. *What Is Posthumanism?* Minneapolis: University of Minnesota Press, 2010.

Wolff, Daniel. *How Lincoln Learned to Read.* New York: Bloomsbury, 2009.

Wollstonecraft, Mary. *A Vindication of the Rights of Woman.* Mineola, NY: Dover Publications, 1996.

Wood, Peter. "Rick Santorum Is Right." *Chronicle of Higher Education*, February 2012.

Woodmansee, Martha, and Mark Osteen, ed. *The New Economic Criticism: Studies at the Intersection of Literature and Economics.* London: Routledge, 1999.

Woodward, Kathleen. "The Future of the Humanities in the Present and in Public." *Daedalus* 138, no. 1 (2009): 110–23.

Wright, Jonathan B. *Ethics in Economics: An Introduction to Moral Frameworks.* Stanford: Stanford University Press, 2015.

Yanofsky, Noson S. *The Outer Limits of Reason: What Science, Mathematics, and Logic Cannot Tell Us.* Cambridge, MA: MIT Press, 2013.

Zelizer, Barbie, ed. *Making the University Matter.* New York: Routledge, 2011.

Žižek, Slavoj, and Glyn Daly. Conversations with Žižek. Cambridge: Polity Press, 2004.

_____. *Living in the End Times.* London: Verso, 2010.

Zunshine, Lisa. *Introduction to Cognitive Cultural Studies.* Baltimore: Johns Hopkins University Press, 2010.

_____. *Why We Read Fiction: Theory of Mind and the Novel.* Columbus: The Ohio State University Press, 2006.

Index

About the Author

Eric Touya de Marenne is associate professor of French. He received his DEA in Comparative Literature at the Université de Paris IV, Sorbonne, and his PhD in Romance Languages and Literatures at the University of Chicago. He is currently interim director of the Language & International Trade program. His research and teaching interests include nineteenth-to-twenty-first-century French and Francophone Literature and Culture, and interdisciplinary approaches to literature, art, media, theory, culture, economics, ethics, and society. He is the author of *Musique et poétique à l'âge du symbolisme* (2005), *French-American Relations: Remembering D-Day after September 11* (2008) and *Francophone Women Writers: Feminisms, Postcolonialisms, Cross-Cultures* (2011). His most recent research has focused on the importance of the humanities and the relation between the university and society.